No Better Friend

Also by Elke Gazzara:

Madison Avenue Maxi

No Better Friend

Celebrities and the Dogs They Love

Compiled and edited by Elke Gazzara

Lyons Press
Guilford, Connecticut
An imprint of Globe Pequot Press

Lyons Press is an imprint of Globe Pequot Press.

Text design: Lisa Reneson
Layout artist: Justin Marciano
Project editor: Ellen Urban

Library of Congress Cataloging-in-Publication Data

Gazzara, Elke.
  No better friend : celebrities and the dogs they love / compiled and edited by Elke Gazzara.
    pages cm
  ISBN 978-0-7627-8374-8 (hardback)
  1. Dogs—Anecdotes. 2. Celebrities—Anecdotes. 3. Dog owners—Anecdotes. 4. Human-animal relationships—Anecdotes. 5. Dogs—Portraits. 6. Celebrities—Portraits. I. Title.
  SF426.2.G393 2013
  636.7—dc23

                                                      2013022666

Printed in the United States of America

10 9 8 7 6 5 4 3 2 1

To the memory of my best friend and husband of thirty years, Ben, and our beloved Maxi.

You will both remain in my heart forever.

Contents

Introduction: SOUTH BEACH

January isn't the most pleasant month for a little dachshund in New York City, especially a short-haired one like Maxi. Rain, snow, and the cold keep those little legs busy jumping puddles and dodging slush. Unlike rugged New Yorkers, with their boots and galoshes, our furry-pawed friends have to bear the winters barefoot—and that nasty sidewalk salt isn't good for their feet. My husband, actor Ben Gazzara, kept the rest of Maxi bundled in warm sweaters and fuzzy coats, just like us. But often, when we returned home and took off her clothes, sometimes damp and city-soaked underneath, we discovered what a trooper she really was—always joining us on our trips around the city (sometimes hidden in her traveling bag at places that were not dog-friendly), never complaining, rain or shine.

Not surprisingly, no one was happier than Maxi when we left Madison Avenue in Manhattan for Ocean Drive in South Beach, for a promotional tour in January and February for my book about her, *Madison Avenue Maxi*. The book tells the story of our beloved little dog and the profound impact she had on our lives. You might call it my valentine to Maxi, a moving tribute to an extraordinary dachshund. Although Maxi has since passed on, her memory remains with me always, nowhere more so than in that book.

On the very first evening in Florida, we had a festive dinner sitting under the stars on Lincoln Road. Two of our friends, acclaimed novelist Russell Banks and his wife, the celebrated poet Chase Twichell, joined us. Ben and I had met them in Monte Carlo. As usual, we talked a lot about movies and books, and then the conversation turned to dogs, Maxi in particular. She somehow always became the center of attention—even when she wasn't. She had a special way of commanding attention. Besides, dogs had been on my mind a lot lately. I'd spent a considerable amount of time talking about *Madison Avenue Maxi* with other dog lovers at book events, and I mentioned to Russell, almost casually, that my next book might be about other people's dogs. Everyone I'd spoken with had personal stories to share. Russell and Chase loved the idea, and even promised me a story themselves. That inspired me to go to work.

When I got back to New York, I compiled a list of famous people I knew who owned or might own dogs. During my long marriage to Ben, I've had the pleasure of meeting countless celebrities from the various worlds of art, entertainment, and politics: actors, designers, directors (both film and theater), elected officials, journalists, novelists, painters, and more—many with dogs that they adored and loved to talk about, just like me.

So I began making phone calls, and the response soon pleased me. People I knew, and even those I didn't, who all had busy lives, were willing to take the time to talk or write about their pooches. In the end, more than fifty people contributed their fond recollections to *No Better Friend.* As you'll see, their stories and photographs make it clear that for many of us, nothing in the world grabs hold of our hearts so completely as do those four-legged friends, our gentle and faithful dogs.

I am happily donating a portion of the proceeds from the sale of this book to support animals looking for homes through the ASPCA, and if this book moves just one reader to rescue or adopt an abandoned or homeless dog, he or she would be so thankful, and I would be so proud.

Elke Gazzara

No Better Friend

Russell Banks

The best-selling author of numerous highly acclaimed novels, including *Affliction, Cloudsplitter, Continental Drift, The Darling, Lost Memory of Skin, Rule of the Bone,* and *The Sweet Hereafter,* Russell Banks is past president of the International Parliament of Writers and a member of the American Academy of Arts and Letters. He has won many awards for his work, including the Ambassador Book Award, American Book Award, Commonwealth Writers' Prize, John Dos Passos Prize, and more. Years ago, Prince Albert of Monaco invited both Banks and Ben to an international literary event, and we met there at the Hôtel Hermitage Monte-Carlo.

COURTESY OF RUSSELL BANKS

Kili jealously guarding Russell Banks

I'm not a Muslim or a fundamentalist Mormon, nor was meant to be, and all my adult life I have been what's called a serial monogamist—a man with only one wife at a time. That is, until Kili came into my life. We got Kili, a Border collie / Australian shepherd mix, as a puppy. My main wife, Chase, has written about this event elsewhere, so I won't go into Kili's provenance here. From the day we brought her home, Kili was headstrong, bossy, emotionally intense, and highly intelligent (a little like my main wife). She made it very quickly clear to both of us that she regarded Chase as competition in the contest for main wife, a contest that Chase and I hadn't realized existed. As far as we were concerned, it had never been a position up for grabs.

It began with a tussle between the two, Chase and Kili, over who got to sit in the passenger seat of the car when I was driving. The backseat, Kili seemed to think, was for the second wife. I drive a station wagon, and from Kili's perspective, the back of the car was strictly for cargo and for less-interesting and -attractive dogs, which is to say, the other dog, her mother, Nan, who is in no way uninteresting or not fully as attractive as Kili. She refused to go there unless I publicly humiliated her by picking her up and lifting her over the tailgate, after which she sulked, ears lowered, refusing to meet my gaze. Then, as soon as I got into the car myself, she scrambled over the backseat, squirmed her way into the front between me and Chase, pointedly squeezed Chase aside, laid her paw across my arm in a proprietary way, and give Chase a snarky triumphant smile that said, *Next time, honey, make it easy on yourself and get in back.*

Finally I installed a custom-made steel barrier between the cargo area and the rear seat, but Kili still made it clear that she was insulted by having to ride back there and was doing it only under duress. If Chase and I didn't move fast enough—if I didn't put Kili into the back beforehand—as soon as the front passenger door opened, she would dart past Chase and take the main wife's position, obliging us once again to establish who was entitled to sit there and where the second wife sat.

It soon became more blatant. Occasionally I take an afternoon nap in the bedroom I share with my main wife while she works in her adjacent office. The second I lie down, Kili is there beside me—stretched out, legs extended, her head on the main wife's pillow. I hate doing it, but there's no choice: I shove her off the bed to the floor. She sighs loudly, slinks to a corner of the room, and stares at me in an accusatory way, which I try to ignore. Then she returns to the side of the bed, wriggles her way underneath it, and lies there in the darkness, sighing audibly.

On occasion, Chase has to travel, and I sleep in the bed alone. When the lights are out, just before I fall asleep, Kili makes her move. A single leap and she's stretched out beside me again, her head on the main wife's pillow, a satisfied smile on her face. I go through the routine of moving her off the bed, and she goes through the routine of sighing, slinking to the corner, squiggling under the bed, more sighing, and eventually I fall asleep. But of course when I wake in the morning, I'm not alone in the bed.

The competition takes new forms every few weeks. For instance, in the evenings lately, when Chase and I watch TV together, Kili sits beside my chair and pretends to watch it with us, and I'll absentmindedly stroke her head. At some point I look down at her, and she'll be staring over at Chase in wifely triumph. If Chase and I embrace in a standing hug in the kitchen, Kili seems to know it no matter where she is in the house, as if a hug made a distinctive noise and she could hear it, and she'll come running to the kitchen to squeeze in between us, pointedly pushing Chase away with her broad Aussie backside.

I know that as a serial monogamist I should be clearer about the exclusivity of my affections and commitment so there is no confusion or misunderstanding between the females in the household. But the truth is, I'm a little bit flattered by the competition between Chase and Kili, and I think Chase is a little bit pleased by the constant reaffirmation of her position as main wife. Of course, this is all about pack order, not polygamy. That's what the experts tell us. But even so, because of the competition and its mildly ego-boosting effect on me and my main wife, I'm beginning to get a glimpse of at least two of polygamy's unintended benefits.

Carl Bernstein

Between 1972 and 1974, Carl Bernstein and his partner at the *Washington Post*, Bob Woodward, investigated the Watergate scandal, which proved instrumental in bringing down the presidency of Richard Nixon and earned the pair a Pulitzer Prize. Carl has since written a number of best-selling books, including biographies of Pope John Paul II and Hillary Rodham Clinton. Ben knew Carl from the many days (and nights) spent at Elaine's, on the Upper East Side.

Carl Bernstein and Stella

There were three of us, me and two younger sisters. We'd had a dog earlier in our lives, but he had died. We didn't get another one until I was about fourteen years old. My parents surprised us by bringing home a brown-and-white dog they got at the pound. She was about two years old, a mutt, but to me and my sisters she was beautiful, with flappy ears and a goofy face. We named her Dodi, after Dody Goodman, a very funny, goofy lady on TV a lot in those days.

We'd had her about a year, when one day, while I was doing my homework at the secretary we had in our living room, the lively and lovable Dodi appeared—and she had something in her mouth. She rushed over to the couch and gently placed it there, looking over at me with pride. I walked over and saw a tiny white baby rabbit, and it was alive. I found myself asking Dodi where she'd gotten it, but she had already turned around, hurried out the door, and disappeared. I didn't know what to do for this helpless little bunny, so I called my neighbor, five years older than I was, and he came over with an eyedropper and told me to get some milk. We started feeding the creature a drop at a time, but Dodi wasn't through. She reappeared with another tiny white rabbit and placed it near the first. Again she ran out of the house and soon reappeared with a third, obviously the last, because then she flopped on the floor and watched us as we tried to care for these darling little creatures.

The neighbors said that the baby rabbits had been lying there alone because obviously something bad had happened to the mother. Dodi knew they'd never survive out there alone, so she'd brought them in where they'd be safe. What a girl. When my sisters and parents came home and saw what was going on, they were delighted. My father called the vet, who told him to keep feeding them milk and to see if they would nibble on a little lettuce. He would be by in the morning to take a look.

Of course, it was clear that we were going to keep these rabbits and raise them ourselves. They would become part of the family. We took some newspaper and pillows and placed them on the floor of my bedroom, where they would sleep that night. When it was lights out and time for bed, there came a scratching at my door, and then a sort of crying sound. It was Dodi, who insisted on joining us. She stood guard all night, protecting her new family.

The next day was Saturday, so we had time to look after our new guests. The vet came and injected them with something or other, my father brought in some rabbit cages, and my sisters caressed their new friends.

Around noon my neighbor appeared at our door with a photographer friend who worked at the *Washington Post*. He thought that Dodi saving those baby rabbits would be a great human-interest story for the paper. For the photo we planned to place the bunnies on my bed and have Dodi lie next to them. But when all was ready and the photographer raised his camera and pointed it, Dodi laid her body over the rabbits in order to protect them. We tried again, but things only got worse. Dodi snarled, showing her teeth, afraid the camera would do harm to her adopted children.

The photographer said he'd be right back, dashed down the stairs, got into his car, and drove away. In ten or fifteen minutes, he returned, unrolled a thin, clear, fishing-tackle filament, and instructed me to tie a loop around Dodi's neck and hold on to it very tightly, especially when he raised his camera. The filament wouldn't show up in the picture, and it would look like I was petting Dodi rather than holding her. It took a few tries before we could gain Dodi's trust enough for her to calm down so it could work, but the picture appeared the next day on page three of the *Post*, along with the story of how Dodi had changed the lives of the baby rabbits. That made us proud, and Dodi a hero.

Andrea Bocelli and his miniature dachshund

Andrea Bocelli

With over 80 million records sold around the world, Andrea Bocelli—the Grammy-nominated, Oscar-nominated, Emmy-winning, and Golden Globe–winning Italian tenor—is the best-selling performer in classical music history. When *Romanza* came out in 1997, it enchanted me so much that I played it on our terrace in Italy every morning for months. His voice is a gift, as is this story of his beloved Alba.

My dog was called Alba, which means "dawn" in Italian. She was a German shepherd, and I suppose you could say I "tricked" my father into getting her by telling him a guide dog would make all the difference to me. He had to give in.

It meant I had to spend a fortnight in Florence, though, at a boarding school for guide dogs and their new owners. It was an unforgettable experience. From the very beginning, Alba always recognized me immediately. When she was freed in the morning with all the other dogs, she raced over to me, licking and barking, then went straight to work. Within days we were independent enough to wander the city alone together. I taught her to recognize the different bars I liked to visit by giving her a tiny, delicious reward each time—and she never forgot a single one.

When the course ended, so did her job. Once we were home, I hugged her and told her that from that moment on we were friends and equals, and that's how it was for seven far-too-short years. Seven years of my youth, which flew past like a gust of wind.

Alba and I went for long walks in the heart of the Tuscan countryside, with her free by my side but never distracted even for a moment, never letting me out of her sight.

No dog was ever able to express its affection and total dedication the way she did. No dog has ever been able to tell just from the tone of my voice whether to comfort me or rejoice with me, and I, who have always loved animals, especially dogs, have never again experienced such a deep feeling for a four-legged friend.

Like many German shepherds, Alba succumbed to a severe form of hip dysplasia, and for me it was a loss of the kind that you never forget. I shed all my tears in secret, then prepared a special little place in my heart for her, where no one can bother her and where she lives on, together with my happiest memories.

Zoe Cassavetes

Zoe Cassavetes is the daughter of two of Ben's best friends, Gena Rowlands and John Cassavetes, her father being one of Ben's favorite directors and his very best friend. I've known her since she was a child, and now she's married and making short films, documentaries, and movies as a director, screenwriter, and actor in her own right.

I never thought I wanted a dog in my adult life. I guess I was still waiting to be an adult and didn't realize that I actually was one, so I hesitated, waiting for that idea of a country house or something where I could have lots of dogs that could run free.

We had a family dog, Cosmo, when I was growing up, and I really loved him. He was huge: a mix of German shepherd and Labrador retriever, and a great dog. But he wasn't my responsibility; I just loved him and played with him.

Now I am a grown-up and live in Paris with my husband. On a trip in New York, my husband called to tell me that we would be dog-sitting for a friend for a couple of weeks while she was shooting in Lebanon. My first reaction was worry. How could we take care of a dog; how would we have the time? I told my husband we could watch the dog, but it would be his responsibility.

When I returned to Paris, my husband and the dog, Zero, a black-and-white poodle (called a party poodle), picked me up at the airport. Zero was really cute, funny, and smart. He walked off-leash, did tricks, and slept late in the morning without desperately having to go out first thing. I wanted Zero to like me, so I made

Zoe Cassavetes and Ikko on the water

him ground beef with peas and carrots in a skillet every night for dinner. He grew to like us very much, as you can imagine. When it came time to give Zero back, I was totally depressed. I missed him. The house felt empty. I found myself trying to play with lots of different dogs on the street, but nothing filled me up like having Zero around.

Sensing my disappointment, my husband took me one Sunday to the *quai* where all the pet stores are. It was puppy season. There were so many cute little dogs with desperate eyes looking for a new home—and there was this black poodle puppy. She was smaller than the others, and she looked sad and shy. We asked the man that worked there if we could see her, and when I held her, she could fit in the palm of my hand. When she went back in her glass cage, she looked at us, and her tail started furiously wagging. We liked her, but we really weren't there to buy a dog. We just wanted to get our fix from missing Zero. So we left this little black poodle behind.

A few days later we were having a nice lunch and, yes, a couple glasses of wine. We decided to go back to the store and see if the puppy was still there. She was, and she recognized us right away, tail wagging. My husband and I looked at each other, and the next thing you know I was asking if they took American Express (they did), and this little tiny dog was ours.

I walked home with her in my hands, thinking, *What have I done?* But she was so cute and seemed so comfortable with us that we kept walking all the way home, where we made a little towel bed in a box. She didn't yelp or cry. She was happy and hopped around like a little bunny.

The next night we took a train to Biarritz where my husband was working. She slept on my shoulder the whole trip, this perfect little cuddly angel. It was at that moment I felt a need to love and protect this little dog—to give her the most love and the best life I possibly could.

We couldn't figure out what to call her, though, and she went through several names. We thought of Nikko, but it didn't quite fit. So she became Ikko, which means "go" in Japanese and fit her perfectly. In Paris, a dog can come with you practically anywhere, and she could fit in my purse when she was a puppy, so she came everywhere. She loved it; she's very social, and she was so cute that people stopped every five feet to play with her, which was kind of annoying, but I understood. She really is one of the cutest things I've ever seen in my whole life.

About a month later, she seemed kind of lethargic. It was my husband's birthday, and we were out to dinner, and she wasn't good. We called the emergency veterinarian. The doctor came to the restaurant to examine the dog, said that she might have parvovirus, and that she would have to go to the hospital. There was a chance she might die. I was devastated. My husband tried to convince me she was just a dog, and not to get so upset, but I knew he was really upset, too. When the hospital called the next day to tell us she would be okay, we were both relieved and knew that Ikko was now a very important part of our family.

House training was kind of a pain for a couple of months, but she learned quickly. *She's so smart!* we thought. *She's so cute, so cuddly! Is it just because she's our dog, or is she really this cute?* She is.

I hadn't lived in Paris a year yet, and I was having a difficult time adjusting to the new language and culture. Ikko became one of my best friends. I realized that she knew me like I knew her. She looked me in the eyes to see what I was thinking and feeling. She kept me company. When I sat on the couch to write, she curled up next to me. She learned funny tricks and how to communicate when she needed to go outside. I found myself watching her with such pleasure and delight, and I was amazed that an animal could make me feel such love. My friends laughed when they saw how easily I'd been converted into a "dog person," but I didn't care. I suddenly understood why dog people were dog people. How could you live any other way?

Is it silly to say that I've learned so much from her—about responsibility, love, trust, and myself? I would do anything for Ikko, and I know she would do the same for me. I get sentimental just thinking about it. She is one of my best friends, my travel companion, my little girl.

Nick Clooney

Years ago, Ben costarred with Jimmy Stewart in *Anatomy of a Murder*, considered by many to be the best trial movie ever made. Jimmy is a native son of Indiana, Pennsylvania, which established a museum in his honor. In April 2009, the museum gave Ben their Harvey Award, named for the film about an imaginary rabbit in which Jimmy gave a truly terrific performance. A very funny man named Rich Little (page 97) and Nick Clooney, a very fine journalist, both good friends of Jimmy's, presented the award. Clooney

Nina, Spags, and Nick

(brother of Rosemary, and father of George) had a long, illustrious career in broadcast journalism, and is now the Newseum distinguished journalist in residence at the School of Communication of American University in Washington, D.C.

After José Ferrer died, my sister married a very nice guy named Dante DiPaolo. He'd been a terrific dancer, but he was an even better cook. They lived in Augusta, Kentucky, a town with about 12,000 inhabitants. My wife Nina and I lived nearby, so we saw them more than occasionally for lunch or dinner.

One day the phone rings, and it's Dante. "Hey, Nick, we're having spaghetti and meatballs tonight. Do you want to come over?"

Nobody made that dish better than Dante DiPaolo. "We'll be there," I said.

We entered Augusta at around 6:30 p.m. on a lovely summer day. Thank God I had slowed down, because my heart jumped when I saw this little fur ball running toward the hood ornament of the car. Even though I'd slammed on the brakes, I was certain I had hit it. I opened the door, and this little dog jumps in and starts licking my face . . . then jumps on Nina's lap, licking *her* face. Then she plunked herself between us. Nina and I looked at each other, and we both knew that we had ourselves a dog. Because we were going down to Rosemary's for spaghetti and meatballs, we called her Spags.

That's what happens during the summer in towns all over the world. People are on the move, they're going on vacation, they can't be bothered—so if they have any conscience at all, they leave the dogs in a small town where chances are good that someone will care for them. We did some investigating and found out that this dog had been seen around town for almost four days and had remained on her own. *What bastards,* I thought.

When we picked her up, she was dirty and had what looked like branches sticking out of her ears. When we got to Rosie's, we gave her water, and she slurped up a lot of it. Dante cut up a couple of meatballs, which Spags loved. She allowed us to bathe her and get that gunk out of her ears. She became beautiful, a knockout. We were like proud parents.

From the moment we decided to keep her, Nina and I began a lengthy negotiation. Nina is a farm girl, so to her a dog needs to have a purpose, must be used to do something practical, and she said: "There is no way the animal is going to live in the house with us. It's an outdoor dog!"

We opened our door and stepped into the foyer. Spags followed and has been there ever since. "All right," said Nina, "but this animal will not get on our bed."

"Okay," I said, getting a soft blanket that I bunched into a sort of sleeping space for her on the floor. But after we got into bed, made ourselves comfortable, and turned off the lights, there was Spags. For a small dog, she had jumped a long way. She started licking away at both of us. We laughed and kissed her back, and she's slept between us ever since.

We travel with her a great deal. Some time ago, we were on the West Coast and drove up to Monterey to check out a dog hotel that Doris Day owned. We had called ahead, but when we checked in, the desk clerk didn't even look at us. Instead, he looked down and said, "How are you, Spags? Here's a little cookie for you."

When we got to our room, we found soft pads on our bed for the dog's comfort, a silver bowl filled with water, and another for food. Impeccable service. All of Monterey is dog-friendly. We wandered the town, frolicked on the beach, and had a great time—Spags, especially.

Spags has mainly Shih Tzu blood, but I think a little poodle snuck in there somewhere. I've never asked her her bloodline, and she never asks me mine. The kids loved Spags, but by the time we got her, our home had what I called a revolving door. They'd come and go, they'd go and come. We were the constant friends and guardians, and we enjoyed it.

Nina's an early-morning person, and I'm a night owl. When Nina goes to bed and I stay up reading or writing, Spags waits on the landing about an equal distance between the two of us. Eventually I climb the stairs, and then we both join Nina.

We always had animals when we were younger, but we weren't as good with them then. We were always busy, doing this and that, trying to make a living. We weren't cruel or unkind—just not smart enough to know how important they were. Animals teach us about kindness, about how not to be driven when dealing with one another, how to take care of and love one another.

Spags is seventeen now—that's about a hundred in human years. She knows all the things she can't do anymore, and she's saying to me, *It's okay. You're okay. We're all part of this process, and everything is okay.* She now has arthritis, but she waits for us, and no matter what time we return home, despite her pain, she runs up and happily greets us. She's teaching us how to die.

Arlene Dahl

Seeing her today, it's easy to know why Arlene Dahl lit up both the small screen and the big screen in the 1950s, appearing in nearly twenty films that decade, from *Three Little Words* to *Journey to the Center of the Earth*. (She later appeared on the soap *One Life to Live* in the early '80s, when her son Lorenzo Lamas was on the evening soap, *Falcon Crest*.) Ben and I wined and dined often with her and her husband, Marc Rosen. It was always harmonious and great fun—but the real prize was getting this story from her.

Arlene Dahl, Marc Rosen, and Maximilian

Our dog's name is Maximilian; we call him Maxi for short, exactly like Elke's dog. He came into our lives about six months after our loving, distinguished Hansel, a silver-gray miniature schnauzer, died. Maxi, another miniature schnauzer, was an adorable black-and-white ball of fluff. He was the runt of the litter, which included three females. Precocious and smart, he stole our hearts from the very beginning.

My husband Marc and I were so devastated after Hansel left us that we thought no one could ever take his place. We were wrong. This little imp was a comedian and made us laugh out loud with his antics. Our hearts began to heal as we watched Maxi take over our household. He was extremely sociable and welcomed our friends with lots of licks and hugs. We were amazed that he practically trained himself. At only six months old, he brought his red leash to us when he felt it was time for him to go out. We tried to teach him to use doggy pads on rainy days, but he only ever lay down on them and went to sleep.

One day, when he was about four years old, we took him to visit Liza Minnelli's silver-gray female schnauzer named Emmelina. It was love at first sight. I'll let Marc tell you what happened next, since this was his experience.

"Liza called Arlene to ask if we would like to mate our miniature, Maxi, with her mini, Emmelina, who was going into heat. We thought, *Great. Emmelina will have to do all the work, and even if it doesn't take, Maxi will have the time of his life.*

"I called a breeder we knew, who told me how difficult it might be to 'tie' them (an expression that refers to keeping them together once they actually do it) until it took. No wham-bam-thank-you-ma'am stuff. I was starting to worry, though, that this might be more traumatic than pleasurable for Maxi. Liza, on the other hand, was really into it. Her vet, a former breeder, had taught her everything, and she was prepared. Liza Minnelli, the Tony, Emmy, Grammy, and Oscar winner, was now going to be a sex therapist for our dogs.

"The next morning, as planned, I took Maxi over to Liza's apartment to do the deed. Liza was ready for action, and, more importantly, so were Emmelina and Maxi, who instantly grew besotted with each other. I'd planned to stay so that Maxi wouldn't feel abandoned as he adjusted to his new surroundings. It soon became clear that this was quite unnecessary, so I told Liza that I'd return at noon to check on their progress.

"When I returned, Liza told me in her enthusiastic fashion, 'Honey, they're just crazy about each other. There's only one problem: Maxi keeps humping her head instead of the other end!' So, what to do? I decided to take Maxi for a walk in order to take the pressure off him. I even had a sort of father-son talk with him. I told him: 'If you want puppies, you can't be humping Emmelina's face. You have to concentrate on the other end.' I brought Maxi back to Liza with dim expectations. I told her that Maxi and I had had a talk, that now I hoped he was ready to be a man. Then I left saying I would check back later.

"I called at three p.m. and spoke to a jubilant Liza, who proclaimed, 'I don't know what you told him, but it worked. Can you believe it? They did it twice!' A few months later Emmelina and Maxi became the proud parents of four beautiful puppies—two boys and two girls. Bravo, Maxi.

Contessa Cristiana di Socebran

The contessa, whom I met through a mutual friend in Umbria, is not just a socialite but also a very shrewd businesswoman. In her early twenties she lived in San Francisco and worked at Gump's as the assistant to the curator of oriental antiques. Now she lives in Tuscany in a seventeenth-century house (originally a convent) atop a hill and does petit-point, covering all the chairs, pillows, and stools in the house. (Her son worries what she's going to cover next!) Elsa Peretti, who is like a sister to her, is one of the most famous jewelry designers in the world, having designed for Halston and Tiffany, and you can find her pieces in museums around the world.

COURTESY OF CRISTIANA DI SOCEBRAN

Baiba and Yuki

★

In the summer of 2004, my best friend, Elsa Peretti, invited me to go with her on a trip to the Far East. We saw many wonderful sights, but the most memorable part of the trip was the few days we spent in Hong Kong.

One afternoon, Elsa and I were wandering around when we passed a shop and saw two balls of white fur and four black eyes staring straight at us, as though asking us to come in and visit with them. As fate would have it, they were Elsa's favorite breed, so of course we went in. There were all sorts of dogs barking, jumping, and screeching, but Elsa's eyes were only on the adorable two Pekingese in the window. They were so small, so scared, and so sweet that Elsa wasted no time in picking one of them up, the female, and saying, "Most definitely, I want her."

I already had a crazy fox terrier at home, and I was not about to have another dog of any kind. But when I looked down and saw this little thing looking up at me as though asking, *Are you really going to leave me here alone, without my sister?*, what could I do? I took him.

Elsa asked how to say "white" in Chinese. It was *bai* in Mandarin and *ba* in Cantonese. So I named mine Baiba, and Elsa chose Yuki, which means "snow" in Japanese. We took them to a vet who gave them their shots, and we had microchips inserted. They had to be in European numerals because no one on the other side would be able to decipher the Chinese. We got all their papers in order, bought the approved traveling bags, and off we went to the airport.

But we had a problem: Cathay Airlines flatly refused to let the dogs travel with us in the cabin. They had to go in the belly of the plane with the luggage. This meant that we'd have to see that they were fed, had enough water, and were kept warm enough to suffer through a twelve-hour flight. We refused, and had quite an argument with the representatives of the airline. They were immovable—but so were we.

Then we heard about an Air France plane leaving for Paris within the next fifteen minutes. We rushed to their counter and were able to get seats, and the dogs were welcomed. Not only did the plane wait for us, but they even placed our luggage up front with us. No one else was in first class, so we were able to care for our little pooches, and they were very happy travelers. It was as though they had done it all before. People actually came up from other parts of the plane to get a good look at our little darlings, complimenting them in every language.

Elsa and I talk often on the telephone, and our conversations always seem to turn to my Baiba and her Yuki. They've both become owners of our homes. Baiba even bosses my older fox terrier around. He's also a born watchdog; no one could ever sneak up on me. With every strange noise, he sends out a warning bark.

Elsa tells me that Yuki is almost the perfect dog for a stylist. She's very attracted to well-dressed people, men and women, and like Baiba, she's very jealous and possessive. If people place themselves in the chair Elsa generally sits in, Yuki growls until they move. Then she jumps up and sits in Elsa's chair until she returns. Also like Baiba, she likes to chew on the bows of women's shoes. But Yuki goes one step further. She is drawn to the color red, so when someone appears wearing open-toed shoes or sandals, she moves in on the red-lacquered toes and starts to nibble. That could be the Chinese in her.

Elsa's sure that Yuki still knows that she and Baiba are brother and sister. She tells me that when Yuki is seated on her lap and she's on the phone with me and mentions Baiba, Yuki barks and runs to the door, thinking her brother has come to visit. Sometimes she waits so long that she falls asleep there in front of the door. Then Elsa picks her up and carries her to bed.

Fe Fendi

Fe is the wife of Alessandro Saracino-Fendi, who works for Fendi USA and is the son of the eldest of the five legendary Fendi sisters, Paola, the former president of the family enterprise's board of directors. Alessandro and Fe are our neighbors in New York City.

Piccolo and the Fendi Family

I truthfully cannot remember what life was like before we had Piccolo, our two-year-old toy poodle. Even though many may see him as an animal—or a furry white marshmallow, as my daughters would call him—he has evolved into a member of our family, a third child in my eyes. I grew up having numerous dogs, but I didn't travel as much as I do now, and I lived in an area of Spain where dogs could have a healthy lifestyle outdoors.

My youngest daughter for every birthday or Christmas asked for a dog, but I was always tentative about the idea. I thought I couldn't give the dog the attention or the space that it needed. Since we travel a lot, I wasn't keen on the idea of leaving an animal alone, especially when he is part of the family. After seeing friends who own dogs use New York as a playground for them, and how they include their pets on family trips, I decided to educate myself and join my daughter in her willingness to buy a dog.

Fe and Piccolo Fendi

Piccolo was just two months old when I took him with me to Paris to visit my eldest daughter, and ever since then he has been to Spain and Italy to visit the rest of the family.

It was only this past winter, though, when I realized how much of an impact Piccolo has had on our family. On our way back from Istanbul, we were passing through Customs in New York, and the officer asked us if we had any food or animals with us. As a reflex, we said no. The officer stared at me and said, "So what is that in your arms?"

As he looked at Piccolo, my daughter Alessia came forward and said, "Well, this is not an animal. This is Piccolo." It's such a small phrase, but it holds a great amount of endearment, and represents the attachment we all have to Piccolo.

He might be small, covered in fur, and walk on all fours, but he is the "little one" (the definition of his name) of our household. When we decided to become a family that owns a dog, we wanted to make sure we cared for and took the responsibility to include him as one of our own. No matter where we are in the world, he is there with us. Soon both my daughters will leave home, but it consoles me that my third child will always be by my side.

Massimo Ferragamo

Son of Salvatore Ferragamo, who founded the family's luxury goods empire, Massimo chairs Ferragamo USA, the North American branch of the company. He's an old family friend, whom Ben and I met years ago in Florence.

Massimo Ferragamo and Penna

It was love at first sight.

The way he looked at all of us with his curious eyes, the way he picked some of us up and called to us, to see who was the most attentive . . . I had no doubt in my mind: He was the one! I had only one small problem. I had to convince him that I was the one for him.

It was the summer of 2002, and I was born that July, one of a litter of seven puppies. I was sleeping together with all my brothers and sisters when he showed up at the entrance of our shack, in the middle of the Chianti region of Tuscany. While I was just waking up to the noise of their arrival, I could hear Beppe, my mother's master, saying to him, "Massimo, you have to take one. Please . . . it will be my gift to you." So now I knew his name, but the blood running through my young veins froze when I heard him reply, "No way, Beppe. I'm on my way to our farm north of Venice, and I have to leave in half an hour. More importantly, I already have two dogs, and I don't need a third one!"

Now I knew that I had only half an hour to make an impression and convince him that he and I had met because it was destiny. I got ahead of the pack, taking advantage of the sleepiness of my brothers, and jumped on his leg, begging him to pick me up. We females, after all, know how to (and generally get) what we want!

Massimo picked me up, and, yes, sorry, I went for his ear and gave it a warm lick. He kissed my forehead.

Boy, oh boy, I was already in love, and there was no way I was going to let this man slip by me. We all went for a stroll in the woods, and whenever he called us, I turned around and was the first one there. When he tried to run away to see who followed him, guess who got there first? When he threw us a ball, guess who went and fetched it? We had a great time, and he said to Beppe, "I can't take another dog, but I am so tempted . . ."

They took us all back home and told us to go in. Everyone went, but I stayed out. They couldn't catch me. I was running around, and I refused to go in! I ran back to Massimo and sat on his shoe. He picked me up again, but I didn't lick his ear this time. I just gave him a nice long look, and ten minutes later, I was in a car, on the highway, going north of Venice! What followed have been the seven best (and only!) years of my life.

When Massimo stopped the car in Belluno, a nice city in the north of Italy, I couldn't see anything because there was a lid on my basket. So I started crying loudly, as I needed to get out after four long hours in the car. The car window was open, and Massimo's wife, Chiara, heard me. "No! Don't tell me . . . ," she said to Massimo. "Do you have a dog in there? We are not getting another dog! You have to take her back!"

Oh no, my dear, I thought. *He might be your husband, but he is not taking me back now that I am here, after all I did to conquer him! I have no problem, my dear. I will charm you, too!*

I got out of the car, and after taking care of a few matters of business that needed attention after that long ride, I met Giacomo, age four, and Federico, age two, my future buddies and soon-to-be inseparable friends. At the end of the summer, we moved to Millbrook, New York, in America, an interesting country even for a German wirehaired pointer. I have lived here ever since.

With Massimo I go hunting. With Chiara I go every weekend into the woods, when she goes jogging. The funny thing is, she and I flush out and see more animals than when I go with Massimo and his gun! I have learned with some difficulty that the chickens are birds that we can't hunt (go figure), and that domestic ducks are different from migratory ones. You shoot only things that fly.

Often I go down to the City. I hate it, but I would go anywhere with Massimo, Chiara, and the kids. I am the luckiest dog ever.

Sometimes, I look back at where I started, compared to where I am now. It's really true that in life there are a lot of opportunities, but it's the ability to grab them that distinguishes us. There is no one like my owner, no one else I could have been with. I wasn't wrong when I first saw him—and he wasn't wrong, either!

Love,
Penna

Gabriel Garko

One of Italy's leading young actors—and a regular heartthrob—Gabriel Garko, a former model, won the 1991 Mister Italia competition and made his film debut at the Venice Film Festival in 1995. Among numerous other roles, he appeared in Franco Zeffirelli's *Callas Forever* (page 225) alongside Fanny Ardant, Jeremy Irons, and Joan Plowright. He and Ben did three movies together, so we got to know him on location in Sicily. He's not only very handsome; he's also very kind.

Gabriel Garko and Argo after his cropping

My first relationship with a dog began when I was four. He was a boxer. I have three sisters, and I always wanted to have a brother, so he took a brother's place for me. His name was Argo. We grew up together, and he lived with me for fourteen years. We had to have him put down, and for me it was the most tragic event in my life.

After he died, I didn't want another dog. I think most people feel the same way. We're frightened of going through that suffering again, knowing a dog can't be with you for the whole of your life. But finally I gave in. I had moved to Rome and started working as an actor. After a few years, I decided to put my fears aside and embark on a new adventure with a new companion. I'd always loved Great Danes, so I got one. He was a big, black, beautiful fellow, and I named him Bacco. We had a fantastic relationship. Despite his size, I always took him with me on the set, and we always stayed in hotels that accepted dogs. He was completely trained, ready for anything. It seemed like we only had to look at each other and we knew what the other was thinking.

He was with me for seven years when I sensed that he was losing his zest and playfulness. I took him to the vet and discovered that he had an inoperable tumor. I kept hoping for a miracle, but he was suffering, and I couldn't stand to see that, so I made the hardest decision a dog owner ever has to make. I had him put to sleep. It was so very hard, but I did it for him.

Luckily Argo had fathered a litter of puppies, so I kept one of his daughters. Her name is Aphrodite. She's still with me. Later I became struck—really fascinated—by a breed of dog I discovered only recently, the Czechoslovakian wolfdog. Now I have a puppy with whom I'm trying to create the same kind of rapport that I had with Bacco. I even gave him the same name.

Each individual dog will always be irreplaceable, but they know how to give so much, and they do it for free. One of the most beautiful things for me is to receive that love and to give it back. I'm sure Aphrodite and my new wolfdog, Bacco, have a crush on each other, so I let them sleep with me in my bedroom. I want to treat these animals as if they really were family. If they trust you and you love them, then everyone is happy.

Ben Gazzara

My husband, Ben Gazzara, was an award-winning actor of stage and screen. On Broadway, in a career that spanned fifty years, he originated the role of Brick in *Cat on a Hot Tin Roof,* and starred in revivals of *Who's Afraid of Virginia Woof?,* which earned him a Tony nomination, and *Awake and Sing!,* which won the Tony for best revival that year. He worked with many of the film industry's greatest directors—including Peter Bogdanovich, John Cassavetes, the Coen brothers, Spike Lee, David Mamet, John Turturro, and Lars von Trier—appearing in *Anatomy of a Murder, The Big Lebowski, Buffalo '66, Dogville, Husbands, The Killing of a Chinese Bookie, Paris, je t'aime, Road House, Saint Jack, The Spanish Prisoner, The Thomas Crown Affair* (1999), and *Voyage of the Damned,* among others. We met on a movie set in South Korea and married in 1982. He died in February 2012.

Ben, Maxi, and me at Christmastime

It was in the late nineties when our daughter met a fellow whom she liked a lot, and they moved in together. To make things picture-perfect, she got herself a dog. It was a sable-colored, female miniature dachshund with big, black eyes, whom she named Maxi.

I had no intention of ever having a dog, but when our daughter said good-bye to the guy she was living with, she also said good-bye to the dog, and so it became ours. In no time at all, a feeding dish, water bowl, small round bed, and all sorts of toys and squeaking balls moved into our apartment.

I was definitely not about to get too close to that dog. The way I figured it, she was only a temporary guest. I was sure Elke would realize that our style of life—moving around, flying here and there, sometimes at a moment's notice—wouldn't make for a happy dog. She obviously disagreed. I could see that her attachment to Maxi was steadily growing; in fact, it was so strong that it didn't take long for me to make peace with the idea that there would now be a pet in our house.

Maxi was six months older when I got bad news. There was a cancerous growth in the back of my mouth that had to be removed. The surgery was long and complicated. On about my seventh day in intensive care, I felt a movement on my bed and gentle kisses on my swollen, bandaged face. It was Maxi. Elke had sneaked our little companion into my room.

Once we were home from the hospital, it seemed to me that Maxi was keeping an eye on me. Wherever I sat, she was either at my feet or on my lap. When I left one room to go into another, very little time passed before she showed up, looked me over, and plopped herself down. I was flattered.

Weeks passed. Radiation treatment had made my mouth an abomination, as dry as a bone. I couldn't get any food down, or keep it there. I lost weight and felt myself losing more and more strength. One day I was in the kitchen trying to drink a large glass of some high-vitamin, protein substance, but it wouldn't stay down. Before I could get to the sink, I threw up all over the floor, cabinets, stove, and dishwasher. When I fell to the floor, Maxi let out an alarmed bark and ran to the front door to alert my wife, who was at the elevator, about to step out for a few moments. Maxi caught her before she left and brought her back into the apartment to me.

Summer came around, and, thanks to Elke's care and persistence, I became strong enough to travel. We have a home in Italy, and that's where we headed. Maxi loved her first summer there. She was at my side almost always, exploring and playing on the many acres of land we have there. When Elke and I were in the pool, Maxi brought her ball to the water's edge, dropping it so that one of us would throw it for her. Maxi loved that game, and she loved pasta, especially when followed by licking one of my fingers, dripping with one of our farmers' strong, red wines. Like Elke, Maxi's a German who fell in love with Italy.

When the day came to go back to New York, Maxi had positioned herself near the luggage. I was talking to the plumber and our handyman. Elke and Franca, our caretaker, came out of the house.

"Ben, is Maxi outside?" Elke asked. "We're going to lock the doors."

I looked to the driveway, where I'd seen her last, but she was gone. I called her name. Nothing. Elke went back into the house to search for her. I walked across the patio, calling, but she didn't answer. I headed for the field, now yelling her name. I walked through the vineyard, but she wasn't there either. Growing frightened and fearing the worst, I raced to the pool, afraid that she had fallen in, but she hadn't. Beside herself, Elke was calling for Maxi in the guesthouse.

The iron entry gate had been left open for the workers. What if she had walked onto the road? What if she had been hit by a car? I pushed the thought out of my mind.

"She may have jumped into the plumber's car," Elke said to me. "Maxi loves cars."

That may be so, I thought. When I called and asked if my dog was in his truck, there was a pause and then he said in Italian: "No, the dog is not here. The last time I saw the little animal was when we were checking the meter outside the wall."

"Hold on," I said, "I'm walking that way now. Hold on, I'm opening the door."

When I opened it to the other side of the wall, my heart sank. Maxi wasn't there. I called her once, twice, then again and again. Finally, from the far end of the narrow country road, Maxi's little face appeared. Her gleaming black eyes seemed to be saying, *I've been waiting for you. Where have you been? Why didn't you open the door?* Our little girl had heard my voice but was busy trying to find a way back onto our property. She was probably so scared that she couldn't even bark.

"Maxi, come here, you beautiful little girl!"

She raced toward me. I opened my arms wide and she leapt into them, licking my entire face.

"Signor Gazzara, did you find the dog?" The plumber was still on the line.

"Yes, thank you. I found her."

Elke came and took Maxi out of my arms, hugging and kissing her and getting kissed in return.

Maxi has been our constant companion. My hair is whiter, and Maxi's sweet, sable-colored snout and little paws have turned a snowy beige, but when playing with a ball, she still has the spirit and stamina of a two-year-old. Her interest in the game doesn't last nearly as long as it used to, which concerns me, but I prefer to believe that it's not that she's getting tired, but simply losing interest.

Leaving the ball behind, Maxi will leap up onto the couch, resting on her favorite soft pillow. Lately, though, there have been times when she'll arrive at the couch and stop suddenly, looking up at it, then at me, as though asking for help to get up there. I refuse to give it to her.

Instead, I coax her, pounding on the couch and telling her to make the jump. In time, she does. I let her know how happy that makes me, applauding her and shouting, "Good girl, good girl!" Her tail wags joyfully. For her, it's a sign that she's pleased me; for me, it's a sign that we'll spend our old age together.

Frank Gehry

Ben's friendship with celebrated architect Frank Gehry—who famously designed the Walt Disney Concert Hall in Los Angeles, the Guggenheim Bilbao, and New York City's 8 Spruce Street, among others—began in the 1960s. We flew to Los Angeles for Frank's eightieth birthday party at the Museum of Contemporary Art, part of which he had renovated and redesigned into what became the Geffen Contemporary at MOCA. The following night, we had dinner with Frank and his wife, Berta, and really got a chance to talk. There

Ben and Frank

was delicious food, good wine, and sweet reminiscence—a great evening. As we climbed into our cars, Frank asked me to stop by his studio on the way to the airport, so he could give me the dog story I'd asked him for. The next morning was beautiful. I wasn't anxious to get back to New York, which was sitting under eight inches of snow. Frank led us through his huge studio, pointing out the mock-ups of projects in the works. It was jaw-dropping. I could have stayed for days, but time was rushing by, and we had to go. I took out my tape recorder, and Frank told me his story.

I was born in Toronto, Canada, and when I was nine or ten— no, I must have been thirteen—Roosevelt was still around. It was the year he died. That's when I got my first dog. He was a little white fellow, a mongrel of questionable origin. I called him Curly because that's what his hair was: curly.

I was a shy kid, into my own world, so the dog became my life. To have this little animal who loved me was amazing. He knew just when I'd be getting home from school, so he'd run down the whole block to greet me on the corner. I really loved to pal around with him. I had always spent a lot of time alone, reading or dreaming. But Curly changed all that. My mother bought him a pretty red collar and leash, and I walked around Toronto for hours, even going into parts of the city I'd never visited before, seeing things I never knew existed. Because of Curly I wasn't afraid to go anywhere I pleased.

But after having him for only one year, I walked home one afternoon and he wasn't there to greet me. I called his name, but nothing. As I got closer to my house, I knew something wasn't right. When I walked into the house, it was awfully quiet. I found my mother in the kitchen, crying. Curly had been playing in the street, waiting for me to appear, when some guy tried to beat a light and ran him over. That was it; no more Curly. It was hard for me to get over that loss.

I never, ever thought of getting another dog. I even had trouble becoming friendly with any. The hurt and shock from that time, you know? But only a few years ago, a friend presented my wife, Berta, with not one, but two Shar-Peis—those dogs with the beautifully wrinkled faces. They were born in my hometown, Toronto, and they were sisters. We named them Matisse and Menina—you know, after the Velasquez painting—and we slowly but surely fell in love with them.

One evening we went out, and to keep them busy we left them with two rawhide bones to chew. That was a mistake. We got home to find one of them sitting on the couch with her tail between her legs and such a sad look in her black eyes. Next to her was her sister, who wasn't moving. She was dead, having choked on a piece of that damned rawhide. We were very shaken and went into mourning . . . until one day when a friend called to say that the very same mother had had another litter of pups, sired by the same father. My friend had a private plane, and he flew me to Toronto where I picked up Menina the Second. Matisse is now three years old, and Menina II is two, but it's as though her first sister had never left her.

Kathie Lee Gifford

Best known for her decade and a half on the *Live! with Regis and Kathie Lee* talk show, for which she received eleven Daytime Emmy nominations, Kathie Lee Gifford joined NBC's *Today* in 2008, winning her first Daytime Emmy two years later. Ben and Kathie's husband, Frank, were already friends when I came along, so the four of us often saw each other at gala evenings in New York City or the Hamptons. When I want to have a good laugh in the morning, I put on her show. Her wit and goofiness always make my day.

Both of my pregnancies occurred while I was co-host of *Live! with Regis and Kathie Lee*, so they were understandably pretty public events. As soon as I shared that Frank and I were expecting a boy, Regis began hounding me to name him Regis.

"*Regis?*" I cried. "I can't believe your parents named you that." But Regis never let up. Eventually we named our son Cody, and for a while the whole subject disappeared. That is, until three years later when I once again announced I was pregnant—this time with a girl.

"Regina!" Regis pleaded. "You gotta name her Regina."

Once again I refused even to consider it, and we named our beautiful daughter Cassidy. Regis was relentless, though. "Cody and Cassidy—what is that? Some freakin' Wild West Show?" Exasperated, I finally said, "If I rescue some mutt from the pound and name him Regis, will you get off my back?"

I thought he'd be offended by such an offer, but I couldn't have been more wrong.

Kathie Lee takes a break with Lola, Bambino, and Louis.

"You'd do that for me?" he responded, genuinely honored.

So I had no choice but to do exactly that. We arranged to play the Doggy Dating Game on our TV show, and three scroungy mutts from a pound in New Jersey came to the studio. I asked a question like, "Do you like to lick weird things?" and the camera got a close-up of one of the dog's faces for its reaction. It was a very funny segment, but I ended up falling hopelessly in love with the puppy that looked like a Labrador / husky / German shepherd mix. He came home to Connecticut with me, we named him Regis Champagne Gifford, and he joined our two kids and two bichon frises, Chardonnay and Chablis, as one of the family.

Well, Regis the dog was about as perfect a pet as any animal could be. It didn't matter that we spent $10,000 getting rid of his mange and fungus. He was worth every penny, and then some. A sweeter, more loving, more grateful creature you could never imagine.

Regis lived with us for fourteen years. He gave us endless hours of devotion and happiness until finally a cancer spread through his body and we had to say good-bye. I held him in my arms the morning I knew I'd never see him again and left for the *Today* show, holding back tears. Frank called me a few hours later and told me that Regis had died peacefully in his arms, looking at him with those big trusting eyes until he finally closed them for the last time.

We still miss him, and every time we get together with Regis— the man—he still talks about his furry namesake, and I thank him again for the greatest friend a family could ever have.

Winston Groom and his dog

Winston Groom

In the early 1980s, novelist Winston Groom, part of the Elaine's group, invited us to spend a weekend in a house that he'd rented in East Hampton. A few years later he wrote a book that, a handful of years after that, became a popular film starring Tom Hanks. You might have heard of it—*Forrest Gump*. On one of his trips to New York, I got hold of Winston and wouldn't let go until he offered this sweet story.

Once I wrote a story about a big old English sheepdog named Only. I imagined he had gotten terribly lost, far from home, and wandered way out to a little village in Ohio, where he lived on scraps that people gave him. He was old and tired and missed his family, especially the little children. After a while, he began making the rounds with Jake, the village postman, which had become the best part of his day.

Only came to understand there was no mail delivery on Sundays, but one snowy midweek morning, when he went to meet the postman, he found the post office locked and no Jake in sight. Out of habit, Only started on the rounds alone. The houses were brightly decorated, with smoke coming from their chimneys, but no one seemed to be at home.

He stumbled through the storm until he came to a small church and heard the sound of singing. He was freezing cold and hungry and tired, so he nosed open the door. The whole village was there. It was Christmas, the pews decorated with wreaths of fir.

He ambled down the aisle, stood before the altar, shook the snow from his shaggy coat, and lay down before the congregation. The pastor was reading a story from the Bible. It was about a bright new star appearing in the East, leading wise men to some important and holy place.

It was dusk when the church let out, and the snowstorm had passed. The postman whistled for Only to come home with him, but Only was looking into the sky, toward a very bright star shining in the East, just as the pastor had said.

He gave a big *woof,* then ambled away. Nothing was more important or holy to Only than his home and family. *Well, why not take a chance?* he thought. *It might be the last one I have.* So he headed east, across a great pasture, following that bright star. A cow mooed at him. He took it as a good sign.

He walked for days, always heading eastward toward the star, till finally he came to a crossroads. A large highway sign said, BETHLEHEM, PA. He was almost, almost home.

Estelle Harris

Estelle Harris, whom I know through Bill Jones (page 72) appeared in *Stand and Deliver* and the *Toy Story* franchise, and most famously played George Costanza's mother on *Seinfeld*.

My son Glen loves dogs and has three of his own: Cheech, Chong, and Chelsea. One day as he passed a pet shop he saw a beautiful Maltese puppy in the window and had to see her up-close and personally. She was six months old and already a regal princess—head held high, big black eyes, silky white fur, friendly, and altogether irresistible. Glen thought to himself, *With only a two-bedroom condo, two Chihuahuas and a bichon are enough for me, but I'll buy her for Mom.* So he did, and he brought this gorgeous little creature over to me.

"I couldn't resist her, so I bought her for you."

"I don't want a dog," I said. "What the fuck do I need a dog for? I'm free now; you kids are grown. No animals for me. Return her."

But alas, no returns, no refunds.

We finally named her Zsa Zsa because she looks like one of my idols, Zsa Zsa Gabor. Now Zsa Zsa has become the most important resident of our home. She's brilliant; she comprehends everything I say to her, she talks to me, and I understand her language. Her only flaw is that she's a bit stubborn. (I guess she gets that from me, but even that's adorable.) She sleeps with me every night. She does snore, but her snores are music to my

Estelle Harris and Zsa Zsa

ears. I bought her some Doggy Steps so she can climb in and out of bed at her whim. Her favorite sleeping position is belly-up—nothing cuter.

I have taken her to the beach, shopping malls, numerous parties, and even movie premieres. She's a sensation in public. Everyone who sees her becomes a fan. But she and I are most content when we are alone, cuddling up together and watching a good movie. What a lady! I adore her so, and always will.

President and Mrs. Havel with Ben and Maxi

Václav Havel

A Czech playwright, dissident, and statesman, Václav Havel participated in both 1968's Prague Spring, the internal thawing of the Communist hold on Czechoslovakia that resulted in direct Soviet occupation, and the Velvet Revolution, which ousted the Soviets from what later became the Czech Republic and Slovakia. He served as the last president of Czechoslovakia and the first president of the Czech Republic, receiving the US Presidential Medal of Freedom in 2003. A couple of years before he died in 2011, the Karlovy Vary International Film Festival in the Czech Republic invited Ben to be a judge, and we were fortunate enough to meet him.

It was the closing night of the festival, and a lot of actors and other international celebrities were there. Afterward, at dinner, people like Jacqueline Bisset, Elijah Wood, and Harvey Keitel sat at our table. But also seated there was the president himself, with his wife. He was on my left and Ben's right. The talk at the table was light and frothy. All heavy political subjects were avoided. We talked about film, mainly, which Mr. Havel knew quite a bit about. While he and his intellectual friends were underground-fighting the Russian occupiers, he, a superb writer, was always in the company of poets, musicians, directors, actors, and composers.

After dessert, we all rose to say our good-byes when photographers appeared, asking us to move together for group shots. When I reached for Maxi's bag, which had been resting at my feet under the table, her head appeared. At that moment, I heard someone say, "Oooohhh, a dachshund." Václav Havel moved over to Maxi and with a soft hand, caressed her time and again. Something had touched him. He insisted that Maxi be near him in the photograph.

"Mr. President," I said, "you love dogs, don't you?"

"Especially the small dachshund. I had one just like yours when I was a child. He was almost human. We could have a real conversation together. His eyes and his tail were his voice. He was my best friend. He lived to be twenty-two years old, and when he died, I cried like a baby."

"Twenty-two years is a long time," I replied. "What did you feed your dog?"

"Very good food and a lot of love," he said, as a tear came to his eyes.

John and Maria Cristina Heimann

Ben and I were in Swifty's, where many of the rich and famous have lunch. Maxi was with us, under the table in her carrying case. Sitting nearby were John Heimann and his wife, Maria Cristina, whom I'd first met thirty years ago in Venezuela. John was New York State superintendent of banks, appointed by President Carter as comptroller of the currency from 1977 to 1981, and now sits on the Council on Foreign Relations. John and Maria Cristina invited us to have coffee in their home, right around the block. They wanted Maxi to meet someone. Who was it? The most beautiful boxer I have ever seen.

John and Maria Cristina Heimann and their lothario Flynn

Maria Cristina said that walking in Central Park one day, this young, muscular, healthy animal kept following them and wouldn't leave their side, even when they left the park, crossed Fifth Avenue, and got right to the door of their apartment building.

"The dog had a collar but no tag, and he seemed so sad and lost that we took him home," said John. "We did look for the owner—put signs up all over town, made phone calls—but no luck."

"Of course, it didn't take long to decide to keep him," said Maria Cristina. "He was a lively, frisky dog, and loved the girls."

John added: "When being walked, he headed straight for every bitch that he saw. He would sniff and gently nuzzle them. He had 'the touch,' so we named him Flynn, after the handsome movie star of the 1940s, Errol Flynn, famous for his love of the girls, especially young ones."

Maxi wasn't young and she was tiny, but also very pretty, with beautiful eyes. We saw in the way Flynn looked at her that he was interested, even smitten—but he had a problem: Maxi didn't like other dogs getting too close to her, especially big ones. When Flynn saw her, he made his move—which was quickly met with snarling and barking. He walked away and lay down, biding his time, as all great suitors do. Slowly but surely Maxi was drawn to him. They sniffed around, did what looked like some kissing, and before we knew it they were cavorting together. Flynn and Maxi soon disappeared as he took her on a tour of every room in the apartment.

Joe Helman

Joe Helman—the famous art dealer and gallerist who has shown and sold work by Joe Andoe, William Baziotes, Katherine Bowling, Joseph Cornell, Lawrence Gipe, Ellsworth Kelly, Roy Lichtenstein, Robert Rauschenberg, Jose Maria Sicilia, and others—and his wife, Ursula, have a home next to ours, both in Umbria and in New York. Their dog, Foxy, was an old friend of Maxi's. This is their story, as told by Joe.

We didn't get Foxy; Foxy got us.

One day I was walking around our property in Todi, and there was this little dog looking at me from about fifty feet away. I stopped, then the dog stopped—we both froze. Then I moved a little bit toward her, and she moved a little bit away, so I stopped. I sat there on a wall. She wouldn't come very close to me, but I could see that she was hungry and thirsty, so I stepped inside the house and got a little piece of prosciutto or something like that, and I put it down. Then I stepped back, and after a few minutes she went over and drank some water that I'd placed near the ham, which she took away and buried.

After a while, she showed up again, and gradually we established a relationship where I would put things down and she would take them. Soon she started eating things in front of me, not just taking them away to hide. Well, this went on for a few days, and after some weeks she started to eat something out of my hand, but not really completely trusting me yet. She was absolutely feral when we first met. In fact, she was so feral that she was eating raw

Joe Helman and Foxy, who is proudly wearing her collar

olives and wild fruit and roots from the yard. This was a young dog, so she was pretty smart to have lived in the wild; somehow she had learned how to survive that way.

Eventually, I started feeding her closer and closer to the inside of the house, and after a time she came in the door a little bit to get the food from inside. But she never let anybody get between her and the door. If somebody came into the room, she ran outside.

It took more than a month for her to trust me enough to allow me to stay in the house with her with the door closed. She slowly overcame her fear, and within a couple of months she began spending the night inside our home. She always knew what to do, where to potty, and all that. She's not a big dog, but she has long legs, and that makes her fast. There was a time when she just ran and ran from anyone trying to touch her, but now she's enormously affectionate, very loyal, and loving.

Our other dog, Ashley, must have been about twelve when he met Foxy. He was elderly, but they still had a very good relationship, though sometimes a bit tentative. They became a couple, although they had no children.

Foxy's proudest day was when she got her first collar with a little name tag on it. She quickly figured out that she finally had a home. She must have seen other dogs with collars, so she wore it like a diamond necklace that you would buy your wife. She was really proud of it, and happy to have a home and a pact that this attachment represented. Every night when Foxy comes into our room, I take her collar off, and in the morning she won't leave the bedroom until I put it on. It's become a lovely habit.

Her breed is called Volpino, which means "little wolf or fox." She looks like a little fox, with red-colored fox hair and pointed ears, which is why we named her Foxy. She's very clever and a foxy lady. It's actually a miracle to have such a nice dog walk into your life. You don't have to go out and find it; you're not making it happen. The fact that good fortune comes your way either happens or doesn't happen. We're glad she happened to us.

Carolina Herrera

Getting her start in Emilio Pucci's Caracas boutique, Carolina Herrera rose to international fashion fame in the 1970s before Diana Vreeland, then head editor of *Vogue* (on the cover of which Herrera appeared seven times), suggested that she create her own line. Among many other notable commissions over the years, Jacqueline Onassis commissioned Herrera to design her dress for the wedding of her daughter, Caroline, in 1986. King Juan Carlos presented her with Spain's Gold Medal for Merit in the Fine Arts in 2002, and in 2008 the Council of Fashion Designers of America awarded her its Lifetime Achievement Award. Carolina and I met some twenty years ago at La Goulue Restaurant on the Upper East Side, where she often dined with her husband. When we saw each other again, not long after at a friend's party at The Plaza Hotel, I knew we would be good friends.

I don't remember my life without a beloved dog. Through the years, I've had a few outstanding dogs. I am going to tell you about Alfonso. He was a black toy poodle, who died after seventeen years of great love, loyalty, and friendship. He arrived in my life when I moved to New York. Alfonso helped me more for this extraordinary change in my life, and he was my first great American collaborator. He was given to me by Deborah Hughes, director of public relations in my company. Alfonso went everywhere with me. We went on many trips together. Whenever I was going on a trip, I would ask for my suitcases, and he would know that he

Carolina Herrera and Alfonso share a moment on a New York sidewalk.

was coming with me. He waited for the suitcases, and, excited, he would jump on top of his. I had to be very careful of what I said in front of him as he recognized more than thirty words. When I wanted to brush him and I mentioned the word "brush," he immediately disappeared.

We humans are superior beings only because we inspire the loyalty and friendship of dogs.

Cady Huffman

In the summer of 2008, Ben was filming in Sicily, where we spent four weeks. Paul Sorvino was also in the picture. When they saw each other in the lobby of our hotel, there was a lot of hugging and cheek kissing. They had known each other a long time. Actor Linus Huffman, another of Paul's friends, had flown in to visit, and what do you know? He got his sister, Cady, to give me her story. In addition to the award-winning theater work that she mentions below, she has also appeared in the feature films *The Nanny Diaries* and *The Company Men*, as well as TV shows *Curb Your Enthusiasm* and *The Good Wife*, and she regularly judges for *Iron Chef America*. She is a woman of many talents!

Cady Huffman and Wilma taking a nap

In 1993, I was a newlywed, living in Encinitas, California, just north of San Diego. I had moved from New York City after my Tony Award–nominated success in *The Will Rogers Follies*, and my acting career was going well. My new husband's law practice was in San Diego, I was eager to pursue my career on the West Coast, and we had fallen in love with two cats and our small house. Now we wanted a big dog to finish the family, so I went to the local Humane Society to find one.

There were plenty of wonderful dogs, but a year-old Rottie/ Lab mix named Oprah caught my eye. She had been in the kennel for about a month, and she was both scared and quite scary. She snarled and barked and cowered in the back of her cage. Despite this behavior, I felt I had to meet her, even though I figured she was likely too damaged to be an easily managed pet.

I asked to see Oprah and patiently waited in the meeting area. My heart melted when they brought her in. She was the prettiest dog I had ever seen: a beautiful copper and black Rottweiler with some Lab blood. She also had a slim, girlie figure that I couldn't resist. With her head down and tail between her legs, she slunk over to me, and we fell in love. I wanted Oprah and called my husband to tell him so. Over the phone I heard him sigh with experienced resignation and give in. We would give her a try.

About a week later, it was raining hard as I drove over to the shelter in my little Ford pickup to take Oprah home on that cold day. Like any reasonable dog, she was scared and wouldn't get into my truck, so I lifted sixty pounds of soggy, frightened dog into the cab, and we shivered together on the way home.

After spending the afternoon cuddling and getting to know each other, I found that thankfully Oprah was housebroken. She was so ladylike and polite. I wondered if she'd ever had the chance simply to play. When my husband arrived home from work, she cowered again. He sweetly crawled on all fours, his beautiful suit gathering dog hair as he went, rolled over, and made simple doggy friends with her. It worked like a charm.

I'm not sure what happened to Oprah as a puppy, but she flinched when petted and looked back suspiciously. When anyone approached her from the rear, she seemed to be very sure that a swat on the bottom was just moments away. We decided to change her name to Wilma, after Wilma Rudolph, who overcame poverty and polio to become an Olympic champion. We knew our Wilma had the same spirit within her, and with a lot of love and kindness, she became a dog that pet owners dream of having.

Wilma migrated east to New Jersey in 1997 when Broadway called me back. Luckily, seven years after we first got her, Wilma was still with us when I was again nominated for a Tony, this time in Mel Brooks's musical, *The Producers*. When I came home with the award, it was her joyous and genuinely affectionate greeting at the door that I remember best—more than all the cocktails, congratulations, and celebrity-of-the-moment glamour of that special night.

Wilma was magnificent. Not only was she the prettiest dog in the world, proudly grooming her paws for hours, knowing they had no equal, but she also had the healthiest supermodel figure till the day she died in 2004, at the age of twelve. She made every move with the elegance and patience of a lady.

Wilma will always be with me—always romping in new snow with icicles hanging from her coat on those days when New

York City looked like a Christmas card, or those clear days in the Hamptons when she would dive into Three Mile Harbor with royal grace and ease.

I never tired of watching that dog play, feeling her nose against my cheek, or having her body against mine when I napped on lazy afternoons. She was loyal, sweet, and my best friend. I've loved other dogs in my life, but it's the timid and scared Oprah who became the bold and loving Wilma that will always be first in my heart.

Bill Jones and Buttons at Christmastime

Bill Jones

While in Palm Springs to see Gena Rowlands, I met Bill Jones, caterer to the stars. An enormously generous and well-known philanthropist in Palm Springs and Los Angeles, he has been involved with the Desert AIDS Project and AIDS Project Los Angeles from their beginnings, throwing many lavish fund-raising parties through his company, Carousel Catering.

Some time before his death, my partner, Steven, worked as a volunteer on the AIDS ward at Desert Regional Medical Center, here in Palm Springs, California. I never paid much attention to his volunteer duties, and he never spoke of them, either. I smiled as I watched him get dressed in his starched white trousers, white shirt, and his brass identification pin. It seemed to make him very proud.

Then one afternoon I received a call from Steven, asking me if I would drive him to Desert Hot Springs, about twenty minutes from our home. Two months earlier, I had bought a brand-new Jaguar, and I thought this would be a nice ride for both of us—until I asked why we were going there. He explained that there was a young man critically ill with AIDS on his ward who had expressed a deep desire to see his dogs one more time.

Dogs, I thought. *How many dogs?*

With my brand-new Jaguar's biscuit Corinthian leather, I was afraid the smell of dogs would never leave. Steven told me there were nine dogs, at which point I almost had an attack. But after fifteen years with Steven, I knew you just didn't say no to him.

Upon arriving at the home of this young man, his father greeted us and allowed us to take only two of the dogs with us: Buttons, an English cocker spaniel, and Sport, an American cocker spaniel. When we left with the dogs, Steven insisted we buy new collars and leashes so they would look special for their dying owner. Again, how could I resist? Leave it to Steven to always be helping someone who really needed it.

We must have stopped at seven pet stores between Desert Hot Springs and Desert Hospital. He walked away from three of them after buying nothing, but he seemed very happy to have found the doggy articles he wanted at the other four stores. With the dogs all dressed up for their entrance, we headed for the hospital.

When the elevator doors opened, those two beautiful animals seemed to know exactly what room their master was in. They both broke free from us and ran down the hall into his room, jumped on his bed, and kissed him over and over again. One dog, in his overwhelming excitement, peed a little on the bed. The sheets were quickly changed, and the dogs each found a familiar human leg to sleep on while their master was groomed and fed.

I sat outside in the waiting room and was amazed as I watched Steven wash and comb this young man's hair and hand-feed him with such love and care. I thought after fifteen years together that I couldn't possibly love Steven any more than I already did, but after watching him tend to this young man, my love grew by leaps and bounds. I suddenly couldn't believe that I'd been so concerned about the leather in my car when all Steven wanted to do was make this man as happy and as comfortable as possible. It was a blessing to me to experience this moment, for I would experience it again some years later when the same disease would claim Steven's too-young life.

They're all gone now: Steven, Buttons, Sport, and more animals since, including my beautiful golden retriever, Winston, rescued from a dying AIDS patient when the dog was just three months old. He lived a short but amazing life and died at the too-young age of seven. But we had a great time together while he was here.

My current love is Maggie, a twenty-two-year-old Siamese cat. Can you believe it? Twenty-two! She has outlived them all, and she just might outlive me, too. We actually keep each other alive quite well. She gets her twice-daily thyroid pills and her weekly IV fluids. Day and night she sits so regally on my bed, looking up toward the Desert Mountains. That's all she has to do for me. I feel she would welcome the company of another dog, and I think I would, too. It's been two years since Winnie died, and that's long enough. Just last week I put my name on the list to adopt or rescue a golden retriever when one becomes available, and we can't wait—right, Maggie?

Stanislaus "Stash" Klossowski

I met Stash Klossowski a few years ago in Italy. He's a fascinating man, well versed in music, art, and literature. When young, he lived with his father—the controversial but admired painter Balthus—for a time in the Villa Diodati in Geneva, where Lord Byron once lived, and where the future Mary Shelley began writing *Frankenstein*. Stash, a trendsetting young dandy in Swinging Sixties London, was a friend of Syd Barrett, The Beatles, The Rolling Stones, and other legendary musicians, playing drums for Vince Taylor and even singing himself. During dinner in his splendid castle I was able to get him talking about dogs.

Stash Klossowski and his dogs

Just after World War II, a family friend spotted, on the quays of Paris, an old German shepherd bitch for sale. The wretched animal looked as if she might not be long for this world and inspired such pity that the friend was moved to buy her in order to secure a safe place for her to die in peace.

Somehow, she was taken to Switzerland and given to our family, and against all odds Tempest, as she was named, produced several litters of fine puppies. In 1952, a fine black son named Typhoon was born to her and became a great favorite of ours.

Typhoon was sent for rigorous police training and returned beautifully trained and skilled in attack and defense. He was able to discover cleverly concealed items and was a joy to have around and to play with. Alas, my brother and I were in boarding school and our mother and her lover were often abroad in faraway lands, cruising or skiing.

Typhoon grew bored and took to unsupervised rambles in the countryside surrounding our vast estate on the banks of Lake Léman. There, with the help of a stray dog, he became a veritable menace to game of all kinds, and the gamekeeper in due course told my mother that while he hitherto had refrained from shooting him, in deference to her, the situation had grown so dire that he was compelled to deliver one last ultimatum: If the dog strayed once more, he would be killed without further ado. In an attempt to avert disaster, my mother took Typhoon to my father's castle in France and gave the dog to him.

My father, the artist known as Balthus, initially was very happy to receive this magnificent animal, but, absorbed by his own work, proved unable to restrict Typhoon's bloodlust. This time, the victims were flocks of sheep mercilessly slaughtered in orgies of wanton killing, much to the rage and consternation of their victimized owners, who not only demanded restitution but also the destruction of the dog.

Once again, a huge controversy erupted, and my father found himself compelled to take Typhoon to Paris, where he was given to the owners of a very fine restaurant, who doted on him and never let him out of their sight. They did take him once a week to the Forest of Fontainebleau, where they allowed him to run, but, because they kept a constant eye on him, there were no more problems. He thrived.

One day I saw him happily ensconced in his restaurant, as though guarding it against shady or dishonest characters. He was somewhat fatter but undeniably content. I was glad to hear that he lived to the age of eighteen. God bless him.

Andrzej Krakowski

A dedicated movie producer, writer, and director, Andrzej Krakowski directed Ben in the feature film *Looking for Palladin*, shot in the beautiful city of Antigua, Guatemala. It was hard work but a lot of fun.

All I got from that divorce was a green wooden table and the dog. The table still stands on my porch; the dog is now gone. It happened over ten years ago, and it wasn't even my divorce. A childhood friend showed up at my doorstep one day.

"Could I leave them with you for a couple of weeks?" he asked. "I have to find a place to live."

And he did—in Florida. That was the last time I saw him. From time to time he called to give me his next new address and to ask how the dog and table were doing, but after a while the calls stopped.

The dog was a mutt, a mixture of a pit bull and a golden Lab. Inexplicably he inherited his good nature from the Labrador side and only the looks from the pit bull. He was one of the sweetest, most playful animals I have ever encountered. His name was Hoover. We could never decide whether he was named after the infamous FBI chief, J. Edgar Hoover, since both had shown incredible interest in anything that moved, except for females—canine and human alike—or President Herbert Hoover, for his love of forests, parks, and open spaces. Perhaps it was simply after the vacuum cleaner bearing that name, because of his insatiable appetite.

Andrzej Krakowski and a childhood collie looking for . . . trouble?

Hoover was funny. Ever a gentleman at home, as soon as the door to the outside world opened, he shot out like a bullet and ran in circles like a tornado until he found a good-size rock or a brick to grab with his bare mouth. Then everything stopped, and the dog turned into a sphinx until I walked out, patted him, and took him for a walk. God forbid someone should attempt to pry the rock away from his jaws. First, as if saying *Leave me alone,* he simply turned his head away, then slowly raised one side of his mouth—always the one closer and visible to the attacker—exposing his fang, a universal warning signal. If that didn't work, he jumped up and, in a couple of good measured bounces, gained some distance from the intruder. With his head still playfully shaking—*No, no, no!*—he sat down again. Upon our return, he always deposited his cargo where only he would know; sometimes he just buried it and entered the house empty-mouthed, ready for a meal or water.

In the hamlet where I live in Northern Westchester, there is an abundance of places for long walks: man-made lakes, reservoirs, and woods aplenty with deer, raccoons, red foxes, skunks, wild turkeys, and occasionally some totally unexpected creatures such as wolves, coyotes, bears, or even occasionally a confused and lost Canadian moose. Hoover got into a scrap or two, but, after a thorough scrub with tomato juice to remove the odor of an unfriendly skunk, he pretty much gave up on his hunting pursuits. The love for rocks remained solid nevertheless.

The day that got us into trouble started like any other. Early one morning, some mist still in the air, Hoover bolted out the door, found his rock, and waited for me. We walked up the hill and entered the village park with its baseball diamond, communal swimming pool, and tennis courts. Since we were early enough, I let the dog off his leash, found myself a dry bench near the dugouts, and started to read the newspaper. As usual, I started with the obituaries.

I was deep into some obscure inventor who had departed this planet at the sanguine age of ninety-seven when I heard shouts. On the other side of the park sat a police car with K-9 stenciled clearly on its side. In our little hamlet we all know each other, but this officer was a stranger.

"Hey, you—I'm talking to you!"

A grossly overweight policeman was marching toward the dog, shouting at the top of his lungs: "Sit! Sit!" Hoover took a quick look at me as if asking, *Who is this jerk?* Seeing me rise from the bench, he obediently lowered his butt to the ground. The cop stopped, but not for long. Totally ignoring my presence, he moved again toward the dog. Hoover, thinking that this dark-clad person was there to play with him, rose. The cop froze in his tracks. Hoover sat down.

"Drop the rock!" the cop yelled.

Hoover shook his head. The cop took another step. The dog got up.

The cop finally took notice of me. "Is this your dog?"

I scratched my head, since I'd never thought of it before.

"I guess it is now . . ."

"Well, is it, or isn't it?"

"Let's say it is," I hedged.

"Tell him to drop this rock."

"He won't, and don't ask me why. Don't worry, he's not aggressive."

The cop took another step. The dog did, too, and I ended up with a ticket. No, not for violating the local leash ordinance, but because the dog I owned took an aggressive posture toward a uniformed police officer—like Hoover resisted arrest or something. I'm glad it was just a misdemeanor, lower-class. It must've been the exposed fang that unnerved the policeman.

I don't know what possessed me, but I decided to fight the charge. I wrote to the court that I disagreed with the cop's assessment of the situation. I was there and didn't notice any unbecoming behavior on the part of the pooch. After several weeks the local court summonsed me to appear before Judge Buchanan. It was a Wednesday, and the cop didn't show, so the case was postponed for sixty days to give everyone time to prepare themselves. But for what?

By the time we met again, more than four months had passed. The policeman's story differed wildly from mine, both from the size and the breed of the dog to what really took place. According to the cop, the dog was a Rottweiler or a German shepherd; either way, the beast—according to him—was vicious. Judge Buchanan decided that the case was serious enough to warrant another hearing. He generously granted a continuance for another sixty days for more preparation. Oh, I almost forgot; he also ordered the dog be brought to the court.

This time we really prepared. I washed Hoover thoroughly and tied a red scarf around his neck. After all, it was a court of law, and we must look presentable. After that, it was back to usual. Hoover darted out the door, ran like crazy until he found a suitable rock, then quietly waited for me to take him for a walk. And walk we did, indeed. I thought that a mile-and-a-half-long march to town would tire him a bit.

The court was full: DUIs, speeding tickets, one armed robbery, and us. When our case came up, we walked into the courtroom, and Hoover, with the rock as big as a head of cabbage still in his mouth, happily jumped onto the wooden bench in front of the judge. The cop, just to be on the safe side, moved to the opposite part of the courtroom. We were sworn in, and the preliminaries started. I stated and spelled my name, then Hoover's. (As far as I knew, he didn't have a last name; he was always just Hoover.) I tried to explain to the judge how I had become the guardian of the dog—the divorce, the green table—but His Honor didn't have enough patience for that.

"Okay," he said, ordering the court clerk: "Write down 'Last name unknown.'"

He turned back to me. "I guess you wouldn't know the breed either."

"A mutt . . . ?"

"But you're not sure. Write down, 'Breed unknown,'" he directed the clerk again. "How old is he?"

How the hell would I know? But I didn't dare say it and just shrugged.

Shortly after that, the case commenced with the cop's testimony: how he was telling the dog to sit down and drop the rock, but the dog wouldn't listen to him. When he tried to take the rock away from him, the creature took an aggressive posture and exposed his fangs. Not one; plural. *Fangs.*

My story totally contradicted the policeman's.

Judge Buchanan took a new and quite surprising approach to this seemingly incredibly complicated case that could have a profound impact on society as we knew it. Then and in the future.

"What if *I* told him to drop the rock?" he asked.

"He wouldn't." I said, quite sure. "But if you approach him and extend your hand, he'd drop the rock into your palm. He's very playful by nature."

The judge, in his somber black robe, stood up, and so did Hoover, exposing his left fang.

The officer jumped up. "*Whoa!* Hold it! You see what I mean, Your Honor? It's a sign of aggression. I've seen it many times." The cop sounded almost triumphant.

"I don't think so," I contradicted. "It's more like he's laughing at you with half of his mouth."

The cop didn't like my remark. The judge sat down, and so did Hoover. With an expression of disappointment painting the dog's face, his upper lip lowered, slowly hiding the fang from view. The judge observed the dog for a moment and got up again. So did the animal, and so did the upper lip. Judge Buchanan first hesitantly then more assuredly started to walk toward the dog. As he turned and passed around the witness stand, Hoover's body started to shake with excitement, his tail wagging like crazy. The judge stopped directly in front of the dog and looked at me.

"And now what?" he asked.

"Extend your hand, Your Honor. He won't bite you, I promise."

The K-9 cop and the bailiff took precautionary positions, just in case I was wrong. The judge looked at them and confidently put his hand in front of Hoover's mouth.

Boom! The rock landed in the judge's palm.

The dog then crouched on his hind legs, ready to play. His facial expression was clear: *If you'll throw it, I'll fetch it. Woof, woof!*

Judge Buchanan examined the slimy stone in his hand and raised it high above his head for everyone to see. "Good dog. Well done, Hoover. Case dismissed!"

Judge Buchanan died a few years later of sudden kidney failure. The rock remains on his desk in the town court.

Douglas Ladnier

Ben and I met Douglas Ladnier almost twenty years ago on a ship on the way to Europe, and it was love at first sight. He moved to New York shortly thereafter and soon became our adopted nephew. An award-winning singer, he performed for a few years in Broadway's *Jekyll & Hyde*.

I decided in my early thirties it was finally time to get a dog. I spent weeks looking online at PetFinder.com and other rescue sites. I knew I wanted a dog that was smart, sweet, and ready for adventure, and I also knew I didn't have the time or patience to raise a puppy. After sending out a few fruitless e-mails to various kennels, I quickly realized that trying to find a dog online wouldn't work. I had to go out to the kennels and see some, live and in person. I wanted to see if any of them would grab my heart.

For the next several weeks, during my lunch hours and on weekends, I prowled the corridors and outdoor cages of the local Los Angeles kennels, from Santa Monica to Pasadena to the East Valley animal shelter, searching behind every locked cage door for my new best friend.

After looking at many, many different dogs of every conceivable breed, at a shelter in the San Fernando Valley I finally found a dog that I quickly named Sasha. She was a two-year-old collie mix, and she was exactly what I was looking for. I wasn't allowed to take her out of her cage to play with her yet, though, because there were still three days left before she could be considered for adoption—

Doug and Tyler

in case her original owners came back to reclaim her. I was told to return promptly at noon on Sunday if I wanted to adopt her. If her prior parents didn't show, she would be mine. I was ecstatic.

Well, a friend had borrowed my Jeep that Sunday morning, and by the time he returned it there was no way to get there on time. I thought surely fifteen minutes wouldn't make a difference, but when I arrived at the kennel at 12:15 p.m. to pick up Sasha, I was too late; Sasha was already gone. She had been adopted. I was heartbroken.

Months passed before I could return to my search. When I was ready, I decided to go straight back to that same shelter in the Valley. This time, in the very first cage I looked into, I saw a long-legged, two-year-old, brindled Dutch shepherd sitting on her hind legs, looking at me patiently, smiling and quietly beckoning me with her warm eyes. I knew I'd found the one. Once again, I was told to return in three days for the final adoption, and once again I left the shelter with a skip in my step. This time I decided to name her after my favorite fifth-grade girlfriend, Tyler.

Three days later I came back . . . early. I got to the shelter half an hour before the staff arrived. I was waiting at the door when they came to open the shelter. I headed straight to Tyler's cage, and there she was, wagging her tail as though she knew exactly what was happening.

The kind lady brought her out from her cage into a small yard. She seemed to like the attendant more than me, but still I knew we were meant for each other. I'd known that I would adopt her before my arrival that day, so I made it official: "Yes, I'll take her."

We left the yard and walked together through the long corridor where all the rest of the caged dogs lined the hallway. To my surprise, in the second-to-last cage on the left, just before we reached the adoption office, sat Sasha. There she was—the cause of my months-long misery, right in front of me. I approached her cage and saw on the form OWNER SURRENDER. Sasha must have been a barker, a chewer, a biter, something. Sometime in the last three months, someone had brought her back for a reason. While I still had the urge to rescue Sasha, when I looked down and saw Tyler, already depending on me, I made the decision to keep the bird I had in hand. Tyler would be my dog.

When I took her home, I immediately introduced her to my neighbors, and everyone loved her. That same afternoon, after I finished vacuuming my apartment, there was a knock at my door. My neighbor Natalie was standing at the door with Tyler.

"Isn't this your new dog?" she asked. Tyler was shaking.

"Yes! Where did you find her?"

"She was running down the middle of the street."

I looked around the apartment to see how she might have escaped and noticed the window by my bed was open . . . without a screen. Tyler must have jumped out when she heard the vacuum cleaner. It didn't take long to realize that she's skittish around loud noises and sprinklers, too. Even today when she hears a vacuum cleaner, she shakes uncontrollably, and when she sees a sprinkler spraying a yard during one of our walks, she does everything she can to escape the water. I always comfort her and try to make her feel better when she's scared, but some things never change, even with all the love in the world.

So that's how Tyler and I began our gypsy life together. We played around in Southern California for about a year, then bounced back and forth between there and New York City. After traveling for some months in Europe and other parts of America, we finally returned to Studio City in Los Angeles to make our home.

I've always had a pretty active social life, but now, before midnight rolls around, I find myself leaving my friends, the music, and the booze behind and heading home. Tyler is always on my mind, and I guess I'm always on hers, too. When she sees me, she wags the whole back half of her body and lets out a loving howl. After I take her out to do her business, we hang out and enjoy each other's company until it's time to go to sleep. Every morning we leave my house early and walk the quiet streets of my neighborhood, something I rarely did before. Tyler makes me feel proud of myself. Her unconditional love is the best thing that could have happened to me. Every day she makes me a better man.

Tyler will be eleven years old this year, and she is as healthy and happy as ever. We go to Runyon Canyon a few times a week. She climbs the hill a little more slowly than she used to, but I tell myself it's because she likes to stop and smell things more often in her older age. She really is a great beast, and I hope and pray that we have many more great years together.

*Three lovely ladies: Pia holds Tosca in front
of a painting of her mother as Joan of Arc.*

Pia Lindström

The first child of Swedish actress Ingrid Bergman, Pia Lindström began her broadcast journalism career as a reporter in San Francisco before going to New York City, where for twenty-five years she worked for NBC as an anchor and arts critic, winning two Emmy Awards and the Associated Press Broadcaster's Award. Ben knew Pia's mother for many years, and he introduced me to Pia in a restaurant, where I was hiding Maxi under the table. Pia and I had a good laugh about it and then shared a toast. She was dogless for many years after her pet pug, Cleo, died. Until one day . . .

For some unknown reason, I wandered into the American Kennels store. I often pass that store, but I never felt the urge to go in and look at puppies. But that day I did. I was drawn in.

"May I show you a dog?" a saleswoman asked.

"Oh no! No, no, no, I don't want another dog. I've had so many dogs. I have lost many dogs. I am past having any more dogs. I am just looking."

"Really? What kind of a dog did you have?"

"The last one was a pug. They are cute—but pugs shed," I said.

"I know; they do shed a lot, don't they?" The saleswoman looked sympathetic.

"And if you patted Cleo, her fur would just fly off into the air." I laughed and demonstrated the fur flying.

"That is a problem." The saleslady moved closer with a compassionate look.

"And pugs are too heavy to carry easily," I said. "I would like a dog I can travel with."

"It is hard to travel with a grown pug," she agreed.

"They are loving, but they snore and are flatulent," I joked, feeling comfortable. The saleswoman moved closer. Her arm was almost touching mine on the counter. "My children are grown," I continued. "They have gone off to lives of their own. They're not married. I don't intend to take care of any more dogs. Maybe there will be a grandchild." I smiled. "Please, I just want to look around." I scanned the cages behind her. "My pug was run over in a car accident," I added.

"That must have been terrible."

"If I ever did get another dog—of course, I am not going to, but if I ever did—it would have to be small, and not shed."

"Yes, I understand completely."

"I do miss having a dog." I paused. "But it's hard to care for them and then lose them."

Her face was next to mine. She looked sensible and wise.

"It is nice to go home and have a dog there to greet you. I thought that by now my sons would have had children."

"Yes, I understand. What color dog would you like?"

"Well, my pug was blond, and that's hard to keep clean. I would like a black dog, I think."

She looked at me and said quietly, "I have your dog."

Oh no, I thought. *No . . . I am not here for a dog.*

"I have been waiting for someone like you to come into the store." I thought I saw her eyes fill with tears. She opened a cage behind her and brought out a small black-and-gray ball. "I wanted this puppy for myself, but I already have two dogs. This is the most wonderful dog. I wish I could have taken her home. She won't ever shed."

"What is it?"

"It's a Havanese. They are from Cuba. She doesn't have fur, she has hair. She won't shed. She won't get bigger than six pounds. You can carry her easily." She paused. "I was waiting for you."

I looked at the saleswoman, surprised. Her face had filled with hope, her eyes moist. What was she doing?

"Here," she said. "Hold her."

No, not that! I knew that would be the kiss of death.

The dog's small body settled against my chest, a little, tiny thing, like a newborn lamb, warm, trembling. I held that small puppy in my arms and hugged her and put my face against her soft head. The maternal instinct is a wonderful thing—even if it is for a dog.

I rocked the puppy a bit and said, "How much is it?"

"Two thousand dollars."

What? I was too embarrassed to say, "That's outrageous! I will not spend that much on a dog. Are you people crazy?" Instead, I just rocked the puppy with a stupid grin on my face. Undone by a little hug.

I'm not proud to say that I left the store with a crate, carry bag, coat, bed, harness, leash, toys, supplements, several months' worth of Wee-Wee Pads, food for a year, and a dog the size of a mouse. I could hardly get it all in a taxi.

When I arrived home, I said to my husband, "I have a present for you."

He looked at it and said, "I can't walk that."

I didn't tell him how much I had paid.

When I told Jack that the saleswoman had had tears in her eyes when she sold the puppy to me, that she had wanted the dog herself, he threw back his head. "What a sales pitch. Come on, she puts on that show for everyone!"

We've had the dog for several years now. My husband, Jack, does walk her, and he even gets down on the ground, and they roll around, barking together. We saw the opera *Tosca* twice the year I bought her—once at Lincoln Center, and the other time, at City Opera. We were so taken with it that Jack said, "Tosca! Let's call her Tosca."

"I love it," I said. "A great diva name for a teeny dog."

She doesn't sleep in the crate or in her dog bed, but between us, silently. Three in a bed is so cozy. Tosca is now six and a half years old.

I went back to the American Kennels store on Lexington Avenue to find the saleswoman who had sold me the dog. Her name was Dana. But Dana had left the store, and there was no forwarding address. I was sorry because I wanted to tell her that she was right: This is the best dog I have ever had. We are inseparable. We were meant for each other. Wherever you are, Dana, thank you for the joy you put in my arms.

Rich Little

The Man of a Thousand Voices made his American television debut on *The Judy Garland Show* and became famous for his impressions of George Burns, Truman Capote, Johnny Carson, Dean Martin, Don Rickles, and Jimmy Stewart. Rich Little had his own show in 1976, made numerous appearances on the *The Dean Martin Celebrity Roast* series, and, from the 1960s to the '90s, also appeared on countless TV shows, including *That Girl, Green Acres, Petticoat Junction, Hawaii Five-O, Laugh-In, Fantasy Island, CHiPs, The Love Boat, Murder, She Wrote, MacGyver,* and *The Nanny*. In 2009, he co-presented Ben with the Jimmy Stewart Museum's Harvey Award.

In the 1970s, I had a weekly variety show on TV. I also had myself a new dog. He was a good-size sheepdog, and I called him Dudley. He looked like a big black mop, and I liked him so much that I invited him to come with me to the studio and keep me company while I opened the telecast. It was supposed to be a one-time thing, but after my viewers got one look at him and he gave them his paw while woof-woofing, they fell in love. He got more fan mail that week than I did.

Proud, I signed him to be a steady fixture. He sat there in an armchair while I interviewed and did sketches with people like Jimmy Stewart, Frank Sinatra, and Bing Crosby. When the interviews were over, I asked Dudley how he'd liked them. Two woofs meant good, one woof meant it was all right, and no woofs meant he didn't care for it. The audience fell deeper in love with

Rich Little and a dog from his act (not Dudley)

him. People actually sent pictures of their female shepherds, asking for the pleasure of letting them mate with Dudley. But he was more interested in a new bone than having sex.

I was married to another woman at the time. She liked Dudley a lot but made a big mistake one evening. Having had one too many drinks, she foolishly tried to pry a bone from Dudley's mouth while he was enjoying it. As she pulled it away, he bit her upper lip very badly. It took an expensive plastic surgeon to make it look like it had never happened. To her credit, she knew that what she'd done was a no-no, so her affection for Dudley never lessened. Unfortunately her drinking didn't, either.

One morning, Dudley and I left the house early for rehearsal. We hadn't driven far when I became aware of a strong stench. I figured something was going on in the neighborhood, so I stopped the car. Dudley nuzzled closer to me, and I realized it was my pretty dog who stank to high heaven. I turned the car around and headed back home, where my wife took a whiff and was amazed. How could anything smell that bad? We hurried him into the bathroom, half-filled the tub, and, because Dudley enjoyed the water, easily scrubbed him down. I even made it to the studio on time.

The following morning, we looked for Dudley, but he didn't come. We called him again and again—nothing. Finally he appeared from behind the bushes as a black-and-white tail trotted away. Dudley's new playmate was a skunk. I asked around and found a skunk-away powder that we scattered around the boundaries of our property. Good-bye, skunk. But we could see in Dudley's eyes that he missed his friend. So for the next few days, we attentively spoiled him with extra treats and games.

We lived in the Malibu Colony, and our next-door neighbor was David Janssen. A wave to him got a slight wave back. He sat there, hardly moving, and there always seemed to be a glass in his hand. It was like a still life. During our game together, Dudley invariably left me, ran toward David, and jumped onto his deck, where he drank from a large silver bowl put out just for him. David seemed to like these brief visits.

At five p.m., it was drinking time in Malibu, so I followed Dudley, who was anxious to join David. David drank vodka, I drank scotch, and Dudley drank a lot of water. I told David that I had never seen Dudley drink that amount of water, anywhere else, at any other time.

"I'll tell you a secret, Rich," he said.

"What's that?"

"At cocktail hour, I put about half a glass of beer in his water. Everybody gets to drink at my house."

Well, what's wrong with that? I thought to myself. Beer contains barley and hops, which are probably good for his coat.

Alas, Dudley got older, and when he was about twelve years old he developed dysplasia, the curse of the big dog. His back legs began to get very weak. He had trouble standing, and other problems followed. He was suffering a lot, struggling to stay alive. After trying this, that, and everything, the vet advised that he be put down. I'd heard from so many people what a painful decision that was for them, but I joined the club. It broke my heart.

Shirley Lord

Shirley Lord's writing career began in her native England before she came to New York to become the beauty editor of *Harper's Bazaar,* later joining *Vogue* as beauty director. She is the author of two guides to beauty and health, five best-selling novels, and a memoir. Her late husband was longtime *New York Times* executive editor, A. M. Rosenthal. Through Gay Talese, we all became friends.

Shirley Lord and Rosie

Before I came to the USA, I lived in Ireland and London. The dogs I had over there were big, important ones—Labradors, Dalmatians, a basset hound, and a South African ridgeback that looked so fierce and powerful, when he ran up to people he scared the life out of them. But at the last moment, he would stand on his back feet and fall onto his back, presenting his stomach to be rubbed. He was adorable.

When I came to the United States, I never intended to stay; I was always thinking of going back. But then I met and married Abe Rosenthal, the executive editor in chief of the *New York Times,* and he loved dogs. He was born in Canada, and his father was a fur trapper who had those huge husky dogs to pull sleds, piled with furs, through the snow to be sold miles away.

The family moved to New York, and their fortunes changed. They didn't even have the money to have a dog of their own. When we visited a home where there was one, Abe spent most of his time playing with that animal. I told him that we should get a dog since we had a country home with lots of room. He thought it wouldn't be fair to the animal because we traveled so much.

When I lost Abe, friends suggested that I finally get a dog. But I was traveling more than ever, trying to get over the loss of my husband. I was also writing for *Vogue* and working on a book, so I couldn't give a dog the care it needed. It was then that a close friend, Gayfryd Steinberg, moved into her townhouse, and her children gave her the most wonderful Yorkshire terrier called Violet. As almost always happens, she fell in love. She told me that she really thought I should take the plunge, and that a cousin of Violet's had arrived at a kennel on Lexington Avenue, where they have the best breeds. It's run by people you can trust. When I saw Violet's cousin, I knew I should dive in, but I was still torn. On a Tuesday, I told Jack, the owner of this beautifully kept place, that I'd have to think about it. He told me that he could give me until Friday to decide.

I went home and probably seemed sad, because Luz, my housekeeper of twenty-five years, asked if I was all right. I told her that I couldn't make up my mind whether to get this dog. She practically screamed, "Oh, please, Mrs. Rosenthal. I would love that. I would do anything." She was beside herself, trying to convince me to get that dog. I told her to sit and think a moment. I was moving around a lot in those days, and I wouldn't be able to take a little puppy along with me. She would need a lot of care and looking after: food, water, the powder room, etc. Luz said she would take the little thing home with her on weekends—that her husband loved dogs.

Luz and I went to see Jack in the pet shop, and when we saw Rosie, we both melted. She looked up at us with her kind, black eyes, and I knew she was saying, *Please take me home.* I bought two sets of everything, one for my home and one for my housekeeper's. I got her a playpen with an eighteen-inch fence. That way, she would have her own space. She was still a baby, though, and very feisty. When I turned the lights out at night, I could hear her moving around in her pen and crying. It broke my heart, but I knew it would end one day, and Rose would sleep on my bed. I couldn't wait.

One night, however, I heard a big thump. I turned the lights on, and there, standing next to my bed and looking at me with total innocence, was little Rose. She had climbed over the eighteen-inch fence. I don't know how she did it, but I went back to the store and got one twice as high.

Not long ago, while I was at the hairdresser's, my daughter-in-law called me, very agitated. "Are you all right?" she asked in a panic.

I told her I was, and she told me that an ambulance was on its way to my home. Apparently LifeStation had been alerted. You see, when I had a hip replacement, my son insisted that we install something called a LifeStation medical alert system in my home. I'd had some trouble with my surgery, and I was quite ill for a time. The LifeStation system was in my bedroom in case of an accident or emergency. You push a button if needed, and an ambulance comes to you within minutes.

It didn't take long to realize that little Rosie must have walked over the LifeStation button, stepped on it, and summoned an ambulance to my home. I called them, assuring them I was fine, that it must have been an accident.

I got home that day at about six p.m. and had a few e-mails to send. Rosie was lying peacefully in my bedroom. My office was right next door, and I didn't want to disturb her. I left her there, not putting her in her pen.

I got my work done in about fifteen minutes and was about to see how Rose was doing when the phone rang. It was the concierge of the building, telling me that the ambulance had returned. This time they insisted on coming up to check on the system. They agreed with my theory—that it must have been the dog pressing the button. They moved the system onto a side table, saying, "That should do it."

It was Rose who made me realize what an important service LifeStation is. They really do arrive within minutes, and that could save a life. I've become their walking PR firm.

Patti LuPone

Broadway royalty, television personality, and recording star Patti LuPone won a Tony for her turn as Eva Perón in *Evita* and an Olivier for her performance as Fantine in the original London production of *Les Misérables.* She won another Tony in 2008 for playing Mama Rose in *Gypsy.* Her film credits include appearances in *Driving Miss Daisy, Summer of Sam,* and *Witness,* and she has been nominated for an Emmy twice. Old friends, Ben and Patti did the play *Thornhill* together under the direction of John Cassavetes.

Indiana guards Patti LuPone from interrupters while she takes an important call on the deck.

My husband and I have always had dogs. I'm a cat lover myself, but growing up in my family, both my cats and the family dogs have lived somewhat harmoniously all of my life.

My family's dogs have been boxers named Colonel or German shepherds named Shep or Alsace. My husband's family has always had dachshunds, and Matt's dog was named Happy. Matt always wanted a yellow Lab, so for his birthday thirteen and a half years ago, I found a female Lab. She was an English breed: short snout and built like a sausage. Matt named her Indiana after his native state.

Indy was the rock and soul of our family. She was pure white when we brought her home at eight weeks old. Docile, she had a dog smile but also sad eyes. Our seven-year-old son looked down on the bundle of fur with the sad eyes and asked us if she could be his sister, and so Indy became Josh's sister, Matt had the dog he wanted, and, in a moment of emotional upheaval, she became my solace.

She was a stoic dog, not terribly affectionate, just a little bit lazy. She often started to run, then ground down to a walk, so unlike a dog. But she was our protector.

We live in the country, and Indy protected the chickens and loved the rabbit that Josh brought home and the cat that found us one winter night. In the evening or in the dead of night, when something threatened the barnyard and our home, she demanded to be let out to bark and howl at the potential predators. But her bark and howl were laughable. It was a cartoon bark that started low and fierce, then sailed upward, ending in a long, high howl that trailed off into the ether. We actually worried about her because of her laziness. She wasn't a fighter; she wasn't an alpha dog. She was just a content animal.

Speaking of her howl, one day as I drove my son and his friend through a small New England town, the firehouse whistle blew at noon. Out of nowhere, Indy picked up the note of the whistle and held that note as long as that whistle blew, longer than any note I've ever held. My son, his friend, and I gaped at her in awe and wonder. She'd never done that before. She rarely barked.

When she was just a pup and I was working onstage, Matt brought her into New York City. She just had to meet everybody, anybody. She pulled on her leash and declared, *Hi! I'm Indy, a dog! Who are you? Better yet, pet me.* Matt called her a chick magnet.

Her demeanor so impressed our vet in Connecticut that he told Matt we should breed her. We bred her with a Lab named Lazarus, and she gave birth in our house to ten pups: six boys and four girls. She mothered them, but she wasn't happy about any of it. A friend remembers that when he came to visit one day and Indy saw him, she got up and dropped all ten nursing pups along the way to greet him. We kept two of the girl pups, Scout and Pearl. Now there were three dogs in our house, and Indy became mine.

Labs are eaters, if you know anything about them. One Thanksgiving I put a tray of cheese and crackers on the coffee table and left the room. When I returned after a brief trip to the kitchen, I found a huge dog bite in a block of cheddar cheese and wasabi peas strewn all over the rug. She didn't care for the wasabi peas.

She loved her car rides, though. Whenever she saw one of us leave the house, she ran to the door and insisted we take her. If it was just me, she rode in the front seat, and on occasion we held paws as I drove.

She was bred to jump straight up as if her legs were pogo sticks. It happened mostly around feeding time. Straight up she leapt, a seventy-pound dog whose body looked liked ten pounds of sausage stuffed in a five-pound casing. It was one of the things I loved most about her. She was a leaper, but she was also the clumsiest dog I had ever seen. She ran into things or just fell over, but she exhibited grace as she recovered as if her fall was meant to happen.

Once, when I was in distress over some stupid show-business nonsense and having a breakdown in the middle of the night, my husband Matt tried to console me. It wasn't enough. I fell to the floor, embraced Indy, and sobbed and sobbed. Indy held her head up and absorbed the weight of my anguish, calming me down. I don't know why I went to Indy. Perhaps because she was our protector, clumsy and lazy as she was.

It's so hard to write about her, though, because she just died after a long illness. She is missed so much. She was the glue that held our family together. My husband, Matt, took such good care of her while she was sick. He hardly slept through the night, tending to her needs. She wouldn't go, just refused to leave her family. She was our protector.

When she finally gave in to her age and illness, she went serenely. She was a noble dog. There will never be another Indiana for us.

I write this through tears, my husband at my side, both of us crying. She was the queen. RIP, beloved Indiana. We miss you so much.

Rob Marshall

We first met Rob Marshall back in the *Chicago* days at one of Marty Richards's parties (page 154). A director and choreographer of stage and screen, Rob is best known for directing the film version of the Jazz Age musical, which won that year's Oscar for best picture. He also directed *Memoirs of a Geisha, Pirates of the Caribbean: On Stranger Tides,* and *Victor/Victoria,* and his extensive theater work—*Cabaret, Damn Yankees, Kiss of the Spider Woman,* etc.—has earned him six Tony nominations. Now he lives in our building!

COURTESY OF ROB MARSHALL

Rob Marshall holds Gillie next to his partner, John DeLuca.

What's in a Name?

When John and I were deciding on a name for our beautiful Tibetan terrier puppy, we had a list of possibilities, but in the end we decided to let her choose.

We had narrowed our choices down to three. First was Cordy, short for Cordelia, and inspired by King Lear's youngest and most loving daughter; second was Sandy—not for a certain red-haired orphan's best friend, but because we love the beach, and our new puppy had sandy-colored paws; and third was Gillie, after the ever-loyal, tomboy heroine (Hayley Mills's first role) in *Tiger Bay,* an obscure British film that John and I both love.

When we got her home, we put her at one end of a long hallway in our New York apartment with us at the other end. First up was Cordy. We called the name with great enthusiasm and . . . nothing. Not an eyelash moved. Then we tried Sandy—*nada*—and we knew then that she had no chance of playing on that Great White Way. Finally we called Gillie, and with the wings of Mercury she came tearing toward us with those bright amber eyes, all aglow, that have come to mean the world to us. She was our Gillie, then and forever!

And so began the rule of the house from then on: She makes all the decisions, and we simply (and happily) always comply.

Steve Martin

Ben and first-class funnyman Steve Martin—winner of many Grammys, the Mark Twain Prize for American Humor, and countless other awards and distinctions—had a good time in Florida shooting David Mamet's *The Spanish Prisoner* in the late 1990s. Steve spoke then of a dog, so we e-mailed him and got a quick response, this funny, touching, wonderful story.

I was fifty, alone, and I thought a dog might be just the thing. I knew nothing about the process of acquiring a dog, and a friend suggested that I scan the Los Angeles classifieds for breeders. I found one offering Lab pups and drove forty miles to a location in the San Fernando Valley. I was expecting a fancy breeding enterprise with kennels and gates, but it was a modest house in a residential neighborhood, and the owners were a couple who had franchised their purebred Lab into some puppies kept in the garage. I was disappointed that there were only two left, thinking that all the best ones had been taken.

I played with them for a few minutes and decided on a bright-looking, well-formed, alert, he-man dog. I paid three hundred dollars for him, collected his papers, and had him in my arms carrying him to the car. Halfway to the street, I looked back and saw the other pup staring at me with such an affecting expression that I stopped, went back, put down the alert, he-man pup and picked up this slightly clumsy-looking, second-best dog. I took him to the car instead, and on the way home named him Roger.

Roger holds court on the set of The Pink Panther.

I didn't know anything about raising a dog, so I bought several books, which advised me to keep the puppy in a crate, a euphemism for a cage, until it was house-trained. I put it in the garage, where I kept Roger at night. When I backed the car out, he sat at attention, center stage, and stared at me with a look of *Where you goin'?* As the garage door closed, I felt I was watching the curtain come down on the last act of *Waiting for Godot.*

I could no longer stand the idea of Roger sleeping in the garage in a crate, so one night I decided to let him stay in the backyard. That night I woke up around two a.m., hearing a sound I couldn't identify. I tried to go back to sleep, but the sound disturbed me. Finally I recognized it: splashing. I ran outside.

Roger had fallen in the pool, and because it had no steps he couldn't get out. I don't know how long he had been swimming, maybe several hours or more. He was coughing, but I thought he was all right. Good judgment prevailed, though, and I called animal emergency. They said to bring him in right away. The vet said that he had turned blue and suggested he might not live. They put him in an oxygen tent for several days; it was the first survival of the many ailments he would endure without complaint, including two fractured legs, a hip replacement, a bad thyroid, arthritis, Addison's disease, and cirrhosis of the liver. (Hey, if I had a drink, he had one, too.) Afterward he stayed wide of the swimming pool, which contradicted his Labrador nature as a water dog.

Roger was quick to learn, and I enjoyed walking around Beverly Hills, teaching him to wait at the curb, heel (sort of), sit, and all the usual stuff. There was something touching about telling him to wait at the curb while I crossed the street and looking back at him, so small and dutiful, and then seeing his barely contained explosion of enthusiasm when I said, "Come!"

When Roger was a pup, I was working on the movie *Father of the Bride, Part II*, and I took him to work with me every day. He had a flourishing personality, and I leashed him up outside the trailer, where he sat and was doted on by just about everyone on the set.

I had just purchased a new Lexus. It was less than a week old, with a gleaming, spotless interior. I was driving home in the dark after work, in a particularly woeful mood, having just experienced the final bust-up of a human relationship. Roger was in the front seat, and I scowled at the traffic ahead. I sensed something going on with him, though.

"Are you peeing?" I said, as I put my hand under him to see what was going on. He wasn't peeing. He was shitting: a wet diarrhea that streamed out in unstoppable glops and gushes. Shit covered my hand, and Roger, now that he had evacuated his bowels, was extremely happy and ready to play. He started wagging his tail in the shit, and, like an indoor windshield wiper, unstoppably flung it all over the front seat of the car. For months afterward, I found dried feces in every crevice of the hand-sewn leather seats, heating vents, side pockets, and sun visors.

Roger and I became best buddies. He was alert and funny, and he loved the usual doggy stuff—chasing tennis balls, chewing rawhide bones, and, when I moved to a house with steps in the pool, we finally coaxed him and he leapt in. Quickly he became a champion pool tennis-ball retriever, and I engaged him in water basketball, using a full-size ball. He swam around me as I tried to make baskets, and he pursued and eventually punctured the ball. For a while, Roger stood on the side of the pool with me in the water while I lofted the basketball to him and, like a seal, he bounced it back to me with his nose. I stopped several weeks later when I noticed the tip of his nose was raw and laced with blood.

I wondered if I could train him to retrieve the morning newspapers. He got the idea so quickly that I understood I wasn't really training him to do it—he was volunteering. The process went like this: While I got my breakfast ready, Roger stood at attention, practically saluting. Then I said, "Do you want to get the papers?" It was as though he had been shot with adrenaline. He exploded with joy, and, after I opened the door for him, he got the *Los Angeles Times* and brought it in and dropped it at my feet. Then I said, "Go get the other one." This thought—that there was another newspaper to retrieve—seemed a fresh, stunning surprise to him every morning, and he again exploded with delight and brought in the *New York Times*. I then gave him a dog biscuit.

A strange quirk developed with his delivery of the *New York Times*. Like a benign neurotic, he took it into the dining room, made a circle around the table, then returned to the kitchen where he finally dropped it at my feet. The first week of this trick was going well, when one morning I felt a slowdown. I went outside to check on him. It was Sunday, so the behemoth morning papers were as large as he was, and he was struggling to get them in his mouth and drag them through the door.

Roger had a special style of eating. He never scarfed his food. Often, I put out his dinner and he would lie down next to it and watch me. Only after I started eating would he have found permission to start himself. He also could make a meal out of a Milk-Bone. He saved it for a while; then, at the appropriate moment, he lay down and broke the biscuit perfectly in half, then into quarters. He ate each piece as though he were attending the queen's tea party. After he got a taste of more luscious treats, when we offered him a Milk-Bone, he would politely take it from my hand, spit it out with a clear *patooie,* and lie down.

For fun—and sometimes to show off to guests—I would say to him, "Roger?" and he'd sit in front of me with rapt anticipation as I spoke to him in lengthy paragraphs. His face showed gleeful attention, as if to say, *I'm almost getting this.* I always broke it off with a two-handed reward, scratching his face and neck, and he seemed satisfied with the attention. This was cute, but nothing when compared to his response when I paged him on the intercom. He found me no matter where I was.

Roger came into my life not at a time of family and community, but at a time of loneliness and confusion. I had just been divorced and was in the dating community, and Roger was there through three serious romantic affairs.

One night I went to a woman's house to tell her that we had to stop seeing each other because I was going to try once again with a previous relationship. I drove home in the darkness, and, slightly depressed, I hung out with Roger in the bedroom. His ears perked up, sensing something at the glass bedroom door that opened into the backyard. I opened the curtain and saw in the faint moonlight a woman's black pump with a tall white flower planted in its heel. I wondered if this was some kind of *Fatal Attraction* artifact. But she would have had to follow me home and sneak into the backyard while I was there, and this woman didn't seem crazy to me. Roger's interest persisted as he stared at it through the glass. Then the woman's black pump started to move. It walked away from the door and across the lawn. It was a skunk.

In the summer I developed a game with Rog where, while I was eating lunch in the backyard, I absentmindedly lobbed the tennis ball high into the air and he caught it without a bounce. The ball thwacked into his mouth with the sound of a service ace, and he ran back and dropped the ball for another go-round. His front left leg had become a parenthesis because of a poorly healed fracture, and when he ran his leg swung wide like a man running with a crutch. This game could continue indefinitely, but one afternoon, after only a few dozen tosses, I realized Roger hadn't returned the ball. Instead, he was sitting a few yards away, torquing his head slightly, mouth agape. The ball had been caught so perfectly that it had wedged his mouth open, and he couldn't get it out.

Roger was about seven years old when I noticed a significant slowdown in his energy. Where he once did back flips at the announcement that we were going on a walk, he now lay on his bed with droopy eyes. Not having had a dog since childhood, I thought this was probably the natural cycle of his life. I assumed the long walks at Tree People (a local park) were over, and I would no longer have the companion who trailed me around the house. It turned out that he had a low thyroid, though, and had to take a pill a day for the rest of his life. He was also diagnosed with Addison's disease, an adrenal gland malfunction. This meant a few more pills to take, so now I had a Monday-through-Sunday pill box labeled with Roger's name. Within weeks, he was back full bore, bouncing on his front paws with tennis-ball excitement. I realized how much I had missed his old self, and I thanked veterinary science and the doctors who cared for him.

During my time with Roger, I did fourteen movies, including *Spanish Prisoner* (working with David Mamet was a thrill), *Bowfinger*

(Eddie Murphy should have gotten an Oscar nomination), *The Out-of-Towners* (with the supremely luminous Goldie Hawn), *Bringing Down the House* (we laughed every day), a quirky little film called *Novocaine* (my second dentist role), *Cheaper by the Dozen*, parts one and two (lovely family fare), and *Shopgirl* (from my novel). When the teamster driver picked me up in the morning, I sat in the back with Roger. If I rubbed his head, he put his paw on my arm. I had trouble knowing what he meant by it. He wasn't out of balance; he wasn't making room for me to rub under his leg. The only interpretation I had for this was as a gesture of affection.

Roger even went to Paris with me when I made *The Pink Panther.* I stayed at an elegant hotel, the Ritz, and I walked him around the Place Vendôme, poop bag in hand. One night I was out of dog food and called room service to see if they could make a bowl of rice with some chicken in it. Yes, of course. It was delivered along with my room service meal. I casually checked the bill to see what they had charged for the dog food: 90 euros, approximately $118. The next day I went downstairs and told the manager that I always pay the price at the Ritz, but this was absurd. He agreed, and for the rest of our stay, Roger's daily Ritz-prepared room service meal was on the house.

As he aged, he became more funny and more emotional. He slept upside down, his legs sticking up in the air like spindly reeds, while snoring and farting. If I raised my voice on the telephone, he deliberately walked out of the room. He never barked, except at doorbells, which made him, I suppose, a great watchdog, especially if the burglar rang the doorbell first. He was a gentle coward, too. If he sensed it was bath time, he slunk away; then, with a little encouragement, he would decide it was a good idea and head toward the groomer. Roger never jumped up on people, and the only time he ever licked me was when I was getting a massage. He casually walked by the table and gave me one slurp on the foot for a quick taste of massage oil.

Roger was ever suspicious when I was packing for a trip, though. If he sensed he wasn't going, he acted aloof and cool and walked away without a good-bye. I didn't know how much being left affected him until I was in New York and packing for a weekend in the country, a car trip on which Roger was going to accompany us. "You're going, you're going," I kept telling him. I took the bags down to the car and returned to the apartment to get him. I opened the door and heard Roger, who, after seeing the last of the luggage leave the apartment without him, had retreated to the bedroom and was howling with heartbreak, which stopped when I reappeared with leash in hand.

In 2005, I was in Toronto shooting *Cheaper by the Dozen 2* when Roger, now ten years old, became seriously ill. Even after a regimen of steroids and pills, I noticed that once again, his usual verve had gone. We had taken to carrying him up the trailer steps as his energy and possibly his arthritis kept him from doing it himself. He was sleeping constantly and fading fast. We took him to the vet, who suggested a biopsy. I was now becoming a bit weepy when I was with him. Once, I took him outside for one of his slower and slower walks, when, barely able to lift his leg, he peed blood. I stood on the street and cried, believing it his death knell.

He made little comebacks, however, and when I dropped him off at the vet in Canada, he was actually a bit perky. The doctor told me he hadn't peed blood, but bile. He was jaundiced and needed liver treatment. But when I went to see him after his biopsy, my heart sank. I had never seen him so flagged. His eyes drooped, and the inner lids covered his corneas. For the first time ever, he had no response to me or anyone else. The doctor confirmed cirrhosis of the liver, and was pumping him full of steroids. A week passed without improvement, and we (me, my assistant, my movie set driver, my makeup man, and my chef of ten years, all of whom had become seriously attached to him) learned that he was having trouble recovering from the anesthetic.

I could see the expression of concern on the doctor's face. He said that he had expected him to be better sooner, but to give the pills a little more chance to work. Roger was so sad and ill that I decided to wait only two more days. I was heartsick that I might have to put him to sleep while we were in a foreign hotel, away from home. I longed to have him back as he was, even for a day, and I was sorry he possibly had spent his last days in a hospital rather than with us. He wouldn't eat or drink, and if we forced food down him, he threw it up. After a morbid week, while he stayed in the hospital, I took him back to the hotel.

Roger wouldn't drink water from a bowl, but he would, I found, drink from my cupped hands. He was no longer throwing up the water, but he still turned away from food. I was given some high-calorie dog food that, impossibly, I was supposed to squirt down his throat with a syringe, which made him cough and gag. I asked my chef, Andy, to slice up some steak. Roger still turned away, even from steak, so I forced it down his throat.

I now had a whole regimen of pills to give him. I devised a plan to administer them and give him some nutrition at the same time. I sliced a hard-boiled egg in half and scooped out the yolk, then laid the pills inside the half egg. I put my thumb over the pills to keep them in place, then shoved it down him. The egg was so slippery that it was down before Roger knew what had happened.

Canada is the land of lakes and streams, and I had a house for several weeks on a serene lake. The air was warm and silky. Roger was still very sick, but, knowing his love of water, I carried him down and placed him in the lake up to his knees, the water just inches from his face. He stared around the landscape, energy-less. Then, absentmindedly, he took a drink of water on his own. And he kept drinking. I thought he might empty the lake. Eventually, I took him back to the house, but he still wouldn't drink from a bowl, so every morning, every afternoon, every evening, I carried him down to the lake and stood him in it, and he gulped water endlessly.

He was still morose and wouldn't eat on his own. We were tempting him with steak, roast beef, cheese, rice, treats, bacon. He only turned his head away. We went to New York for the weekend, where I have an apartment. My girlfriend, Anne, Andy, and I carted him downstairs and upstairs, our pockets stuffed with hopeful poop bags, but he was as evacuated as an afternoon showing of *The Lonely Guy*. That evening in the kitchen, before shoving a wad of food down his throat, I routinely held out the unwanted steak. He took it. We stared. Then he took another one. There was celebration in our group, like Roger had just homered in the World Series.

I had weeks to go before the completion of the movie, so we all flew back to Canada. He was still very sick, and it was possible for him to go either way. Ilene, my assistant of twenty years, and another person who adored him, flew to Canada from Los Angeles, ostensibly to work, but I knew it was to see Roger in case this was his last stand. She drove to the lake house and knocked on the door. Roger was moping on the floor, but when the door opened, he did something he hadn't done in months: He picked up his rawhide bone. This was a protected possession, a call to play, a welcome. Roger was back.

Eventually he returned to his routines with a kind of vigor we hadn't seen in several years. The staff in Los Angeles avidly greeted him. To his list of nicknames—Buddy, Genius, Rog, Mister, The Boy, Lump, Bunny, The Pope, Roger the Dog—we added another: Lazarus.

He renewed his obsessive visits to the kitchen when Andy was cooking dinner. We have a swinging door, and if he was going from the kitchen to the dining room, he pushed it open with a small leap. But, mysteriously, going the other way, he waited until I shouted, "GO SEE ANDY!" before he plowed his way through. This became a ritual at dinnertime. The meal was constantly punctuated with "GO SEE ANDY!"

In New York, I had an idea, a frivolous one, to teach Roger to walk himself. When Anne—we were now married—and I returned home one evening, she went upstairs, tied a poop bag to his chain, and put Roger alone on the elevator while I waited down below. Roger emerged from the elevator, tentatively looked around, saw me, and we walked outside to his favorite tree. Each night, I moved farther and farther away from the elevator. Eventually, I waited outside, and Roger, assisted by doormen wise to the routine, who opened the building doors for him, ran to his tree where I was waiting for him. I knew that in time he could have learned the whole process and returned on his own to the elevator, though we would never have let him do it on his own without keeping a watchful eye on him.

Five months later, Roger was slowing down again. I had to go to Europe for five days to promote *Pink Panther*. We were all in New York, and Anne expressed worry that whenever I left him he became low. There was nothing that could be done, though. I had to leave. I called from Rome; "Roger doesn't seem well," she said. I called from Paris; "Roger had a good day," she said. She and Andy took him to Central Park where he had a long walk and even stood in the lake and looked at birds. I called her from Berlin; "I'm glad Roger's doing well," I said. She said, "He's not really doing that well."

I came home, and Anne brought Roger down the elevator to greet me. But he lay down at the elevator entrance, and when he saw me he didn't wag his tail. He wasn't eating or drinking and was throwing up food. We called the vet, and she suggested he go into the hospital for tests right away. They wanted to keep him overnight, giving him steroids and intravenous fluids.

I went the next day to see him, and the doctor told me he hadn't improved. I called Anne from the street, telling her that Roger wasn't better. It was a Sunday, and I took him home to be with us. I didn't want him to spend any more time in the hospital than he had to, and the doctor said love was the best medicine he could receive right now.

We laid him on his bed in the bedroom. I filled my cupped hands with water, and he drank a bit. Then he threw it up. It was a freezing day in New York. I took him outside to pee, and his front legs were shaking from the struggle to hold himself up. He tried to shit, then he walked a few steps and fell over, weary. Audible sounds of sympathy came from passersby. I picked him up, using him to cover my weeping face, and took him back upstairs.

We put him on his bed, and Anne stroked him for long sessions. I leaned down to him, and he put his paw on my arm. We called the doctor and reported his condition. "Would you like me to come over?" she said. Yes, we said.

The doctor arrived and examined him. He probably wouldn't last to the morning, she said. His liver and lungs were failing. I had hoped to get him to Los Angeles one last time so he could be in the garden and home he grew up in, but clearly I couldn't. I asked if she was prepared for euthanasia, and she said yes. Anne and I stroked his face, and the valium injection, intended to relax him, made him look serene.

Then it was over.

Being Sunday, there was no one to handle the body until morning. Andy, Anne, and I wrapped him in a red blanket and put him outside on a small balcony overlooking Central Park, where the temperature was below freezing. Anne, who sometimes decorated Roger for Christmas parties, found a green ribbon and wrapped it around the blanket. Once, during the night, Anne and I went to visit him. A small moon illuminated him, and there was something lovely about his little soul resting over Central Park, silent Manhattan looking on. His body was collected the next day.

The next week was a compound of firsts: the first morning without him, without having to take him outside, without his greeting when we came home. I walked down Central Park West, reached in my coat pocket, and found a folded poop bag, ready for use. But now it was a memento mori with heart-wrenching significance. I rubbed my thumb back and forth across it. There were a few moments that week, four to be exact, each lasting about two seconds, where, unconnected to any artifact or memory, I found the loss unbearable.

I came home to Los Angeles, to a house I have lived in for eleven years, a house that had never known life without Roger. There his absence was tangible—stray tennis balls in the garden, silence when the doorbell rang and not seeing him run back to the bedroom with the expression on his face of *Someone's here! What are we going to do about it?* The house's staff was gloomy, and we wept spontaneously when we passed each other in the hall. I took his blanket out of the backseat of the car and stored it downstairs, and left a chewed tennis ball I found in the backyard as a shrine in the living room. I am sad, and will be sad for a while, but after Toronto, I did get him back from death for a while, and all those who loved him saw him in great health for the last five months of his life.

I realize this story involves privilege, fancy hotels, household staff, cooks, planes, and elaborate medical treatments. To those of you in different circumstances but with a similar experience, I extend my heart. We love our pets, our uncomplicated companions, the ones who allow us to talk to ourselves without sounding crazy, the ones we can fully love without hesitation, the ones who are our counter-glow. I don't think of the last eleven years of my life as defined by the movies I made or successes or failures of any kind. During that time, I lost both my parents, renewed family relationships, loved and lost, and loved and won, lived my entire fifties, and emerged as a fuller and more available person. But those eleven years, as my emotions rose and fell, had a vital constant, and I will always think of it as the era of Roger.

Liliane Montevecchi

For decades, the Tony-winning Liliane Montevecchi has entertained us in motion pictures, on television, and in the theater. An MGM contract player in the 1950s, she toured with the Folies Bergère for a time and appeared in movies opposite Elvis Presley and Jerry Lewis. She's an old friend whom Ben knew through Tommy Tune (page 210). These days she continues to captivate audiences with her cabaret shows.

Liliane Montevecchi and Stella

In 1961 I was touring with a play called *La Plume de Ma Tante*. We toured for two years, I and Monsieur, my silver-gray miniature poodle. He was five years old then, extremely beautiful, and intelligent. In those days it was hard to travel with a dog. You had to search out airlines and hotels that were dog-friendly. Very few were.

We were in Canada and had a short flight ahead of us—Montreal to Toronto. I boarded a two-engine, propeller-powered plane, carrying my makeup kit in my left hand. In my right was the five-pound Monsieur, already asleep in his ventilated carrying case. As soon as I was seated, a stewardess appeared and said that company rules didn't allow a dog in the cabin—that my dog had to be placed below with the luggage. I became agitated and angry and told the girl that I had cleared everything with the airline, but she insisted that there must have been a misunderstanding and excused herself. Very soon, a tall, handsome man appeared and introduced himself as the captain, repeating the same mantra: The dog would only be allowed to ride in a crate in the underbelly of the plane. I told him I had no crate—that Monsieur always traveled in his own little home. I pleaded with him, telling him that I had to be in Toronto that afternoon because I had a performance that very evening.

"I'll see what I can do," he said, and disappeared.

But soon he reappeared holding a medium-size cardboard box and some blankets. He proceeded to punch holes through the sides of the box, laying the blankets in it.

"Remove your pooch from his bag, please," he said. "He'll be very comfortable in here, and I'll have him placed in a very safe spot."

I did as I was told. We were already late, and I just had to get to Toronto. "Please take care of him, Captain. He's never traveled alone."

"I'll handle him like he was my own," he said, placing Monsieur in the box and sealing it.

I waited and watched through the window as the carton was brought to the tarmac and placed with all the passenger luggage, which was then rolling slowly into the belly of the plane. I was sobbing very loudly, I'm afraid, so I ordered a whiskey and gulped it down through my tears, closed my eyes, and could think only of my little angel. Did he know what was going on? Was he missing me? Was he cold? Was he trembling with fright? Would he even survive? I had never been so distraught in my life, but I willed myself to relax, trying to convince myself that everything would be fine.

We took off finally, and within minutes I heard laughter and what sounded like applause coming from the back of the plane. I turned and looked, and what did I see? A ball of gray fur moving slowly up the aisle, making happy, wailing noises. It was my Monsieur, huffing and puffing with his tongue hanging out. He jumped into my lap and pressed himself hard against me. I think he was trying to disappear so that he couldn't be taken from me again.

It seems that in those old small propeller planes there was access between the cabin and luggage area. Monsieur had clawed and chewed his way through that cardboard box until he had freed himself and found his way home to his mother. As the applause and laughter continued, the captain looked in, saw what was happening, smiled warmly, and saluted me.

Oh, my Monsieur, I think of you so often.

Katharina Otto-Bernstein

The youngest daughter of German industrialist and entrepreneur Werner Otto, Katharina Otto-Bernstein was born in Hamburg and grew up Oxford, London, and New York City. An award-winning writer, director, and producer, she lives and works in New York now, where she met our family.

Dog Days: An Embarrassing but True Story

What all of us New York dog owners have in common is the painful duty that lies in the disposal of our canine partners' droppings. Believe me, there is nothing more demeaning than when you prance down the busy avenues, a gorgeous male has just given you the eye, and your little darling decides that precisely that moment is the right time and place. Needless to say, there will always be some traffic cop in the vicinity telling you: "It'll be a $150 fine, miss, if you don't pick that up RIGHT NOW." Then he'll hover over you to supervise. On your knees, confronted with the realities of your dog's digestion, you look for a sympathetic reaction from Mr. Gorgeous. He, of course, utterly disgusted, has jumped a red traffic light and fled to the other side of the street. Oh, the agony, the agony.

To avoid this kind of humiliation, people have developed various techniques to deal with the issue efficiently and inconspicuously. You have your ecologically conscious newspaper picker-upper, or the sophisticated shovel-handler. I've always

Katharina Otto-Bernstein and Vincent on a less stressful outing

admired the nonchalance of the Chanel Lady, who, with an expert "twist of the wrist," removes her poodle's ugly mess. Personally I am a baggie sort of girl: I descend on the heap like a stealth fighter, and it's gone in the blink of an eye.

At the end of the day, it's a small price to pay for my adorable Vincent, my champagne-colored cocker spaniel with the shiniest brown eyes that will melt your heart right away. There's no denying it—I live life according to Vincent. I would do anything for him. He knows that and takes full advantage of the privilege. He sleeps in my bed, eats next to the dining table, chooses my boyfriends, and I don't have a problem with that. In fact, I enjoy it.

The only thing I dread is the visit to the vet. Of course I use the best veterinarian in town. His name is Dr. Padwee. Yes, really. No pun intended. It's difficult to get appointments with the perpetually overbooked dog guru, so you move heaven and earth, including a visit from your mother-in-law, to make it there and in time. (Padwee has a wait list.) Once you land the appointment, Dr. Padwee requires that your visit be accompanied by a stool sample.

On Thursday morning at seven a.m.—the appointment is at eleven—Vincent and I are walking briskly through the park to collect the desired sample. We are right away successful—sufficient in amount, adequate in texture. Both of us are very pleased with our result, and I wrap the doo-doo first in aluminum foil and then in a plastic bag. It looks like a small parcel.

Back home, I carefully place the parcel on the mahogany dining table and retreat upstairs to take a bath. Down below I can hear Maria, my Brazilian housekeeper, singing to Vincent. Maria understands English but doesn't speak any. I find that very convenient because it spares me having to listen to all of Maria's family tragedies that occur in her Brazilian homeland. Vincent, on the other hand, understands and speaks Brazilian perfectly. He knows Maria's private life inside out. That's why Maria prefers Vincent to me.

After a refreshing beauty session, it's now time for the vet. I am descending the stairs, and my eyes are scanning the dining table. It's empty. *Where is the stool sample?* Dr. Padwee doesn't take you without it, and if you cancel he might never take you again.

"*Maaaaaarrrriiiiaaaaaa!*"

Maria appears from behind the closet. "Whot?"

Silently I point at the table. "Where is the package? It is very, very important."

Maria snaps back defiantly. "Pooh-pooh de Vinnie important? It smell very bad. I throw away."

I am growing increasingly anxious. "Please retrace your steps, and think very carefully. Where could it be?"

"I put in garbage in basement."

While I am rushing to the basement, Maria gives Vincent a long, thoughtful look, telling him *Poor baby. Your mama crazy!*

Down in the underbelly of my apartment building, I run into Charlie the handyman. Charlie is shoving heaps of garbage into a large container. "Can I help you, miss?"

This is obscene. I can't ask the man to help me search for my dog's excrement. I choke, and slowly I shake my head. I will have to explain to Dr. Padwee that I am the victim of circumstance. What a nightmare—why me?

Then inspiration strikes. Maybe if I walk Vincent the long way to the vet he will have to go again. *Genius.*

The Upper East Side is prone to constant change; the rents are raised, stores close, new ones open, the new ones grow old and close, and newer ones open. Some places, however, are neighborhood institutions. One of them is Godiva, chocolatiers since . . . I don't know, presumably the Stone Age. Godiva only sells items to do with chocolate. Dark chocolate truffles, light chocolate cakes, and you can also sit down in the attached cafe and sip hot chocolate. From such seats, you can observe life on Madison Avenue. You can observe it well because Godiva's windows are very large. You almost feel part of the action.

When walking to Dr. Padwee we have to pass Godiva, and all the chocolate-eating people sitting by the window. I'm terribly concerned with Vincent's bowel movements, but still, there's a shred of dignity left inside of me, and I'm certainly not blind to my surroundings. Of course, just in front of Godiva, I feel THE PULL. Not the sniffling stretch of the leash, but THE PULL. (My friend Jason calls it the doody pull.) I should be happy for this long-awaited event that will propel me back into the good graces and capable hands of Dr. Padwee. But here? Now? Oh, Vincent!

Vincent has found a comfortable position, looking with velvet eyes at two elderly ladies hacking away at their chocolate cakes. He has overcome the preparation phase and is getting right down to business. Why does chocolate have this, well, this . . . I don't dare say it. The ladies have stopped eating and are pushing their plates into the middle of the table, glaring at me as if I were the one taking care of business. Hey, the dog has to go; there's nothing I can do. By now Vincent has produced a stately piece of evidence. Good dog!

Dr. Padwee always enjoys a professionally prepared package, and I oblige. The ladies cover their mouths. They are frozen in a state of panic as they watch me placing the stool sample into my Vuitton handbag.

I love my dog, and it's essential to me that he enjoys the best care. That's why I have a healthy dog, which brings me great joy. Despite all the trials and tribulations, in my opinion, everyone should get a Vincent!

Joe Pesci

A young Joe Pesci came to the attention of Martin Scorsese and Robert De Niro before appearing in *Raging Bull,* which launched his film career. For many years he and Ben shared the watchful eye of powerful Hollywood lawyer and business manager, Jay Julien. Pesci also appeared in the *Lethal Weapon* movies; *Goodfellas,* for which he won an Academy Award; the *Home Alone* movies; *My Cousin Vinny;* and *Casino.* He also plays the guitar beautifully and sings in perfect Italian.

Marlon

Tyson

My dog found me on my doorstep. I lived on Mulholland with a long driveway, and it was raining hard that morning. I didn't have an umbrella, and my morning newspaper was always dropped at the end of my driveway, so I ran down there in my robe. I was heading back to my house when I saw something dark lying near my gatepost. It looked like a garbage bag, but when I went to pick it up, it moved, got up, and shook itself off. It was a good-size dog, and he was soaking wet.

How did he get to my gate? I wondered.

Not knowing if he was friendly or not, I headed back toward the house. I figured that he'd found his way onto my property—he'd find his way off. When I got to my front door, I felt something rubbing against my leg. I looked down, and there he was, giving me a look that broke my heart. This dog had no collar, no name tag, nothing, and he was shivering. I told him to stay and ran to the downstairs bathroom to get a big towel. When I went back, he hadn't moved. He was waiting for me. So I dried him off and invited him in. That was nine years ago.

I did try to find his owner, putting signs all over the neighborhood. Days passed, and there were no calls, no visits, but still, I didn't intend to keep him. I called him Doggie, figuring his real owner would eventually show up and take him back. But he never did. I was glad, because I was starting to get attached to him. He never left my side, and even slept in my bedroom. I enjoy looking at him. He's a beautiful shepherd/Labrador mix.

I hired a dog trainer to take care of him when I played golf or something, taking him to the park, the beach, everywhere. One day the trainer says to me, "Mr. Pesci, please give your dog a name. It's really hard, even embarrassing, for me to yell out, 'Doggie, come here!'" So I decided to give him a strong name. I chose Marlon because Brando was so powerful, yet so tender—like my dog.

I know I'm prejudiced, but I have myself a great dog, and one hell of a protector. He guards my house and me, and this guy will catch a tennis ball from any distance or any height I throw it.

He's eleven years old now, and I don't even want to think about losing him. I want him to be happy while he's still here, so I just brought home a new buddy for him to play with. I got him from a pound. He's a big puppy, and very strong, so I named him Tyson, after tough Mike. He's very frisky, and when Marlon plays with him, he becomes young again. That makes me happy.

Bernadette Peters

Winner of three Tonys and three Drama Desk Awards, Bernadette Peters is one of the most critically acclaimed Broadway performers, known for star turns in *Gypsy, Into the Woods,* and *Sunday in the Park with George.* She also won acclaim in movies such as *The Jerk, Pennies from Heaven,* and *Annie.* Surprisingly, she never worked directly with Ben, but they ran in the same circles for years. When she's not captivating audiences, she champions homeless dogs, having founded Broadway Barks, which raises money for and helps people adopt shelter dogs.

PHOTOGRAPH BY GEOFFREY TISCHMAN

Bernadette Peters and Kramer

★

When our golden retriever died and we finally decided it was time to get another dog, we went to the ASPCA, which we thought was the city pound. When we arrived, I was shown a picture of a dog named Douglas. There he was—my dream dog—and they said we could meet him. We went in, and the first thing we saw was a little female pit bull, sleek and beautiful, who looked like a cartoon of a black panther. Unfortunately she had developed chronic diarrhea from a nervous stomach.

Oh, I said to myself. *I have to adopt this dog because no one will want her, and she will be euthanized.*

But this wasn't the city shelter anymore, and the ASPCA doesn't euthanize their animals. They work only to protect animals against cruel and inhuman acts. A worker upstairs had fallen in love with this little pit bull (Rosy, I think her name was), and she was going home with her. I was happy about that, and happier still that I was going to meet Douglas, who looked like the dog I'd always wanted since I was a little girl.

They brought in Douglas, and he was very nervous, literally bouncing off the walls, jumping on tables, never looking you in the eyes. It was no wonder this beautiful dog was still in the shelter. He was only a year old and obviously had been abused. It took time, but finally, with a lot of coaxing and help, we got him to lie down. Suddenly he relaxed and stretched out on his side. I spoke to him gently and asked him to give me his paw, but he didn't. I said, "I think you understand what I'm saying, don't you? I just want to hold your paw." At that point he put his right paw in my hand. We connected, and I fell in love. I couldn't believe that my dream dog was now mine.

We took him home, but he still wouldn't look us in the eyes. I guess we hadn't earned his trust yet. That is, until we gave him a bath. As we were drying him off, he looked up at us with grateful eyes, as if to say, *You really* do *care about me, don't you?* That dog had been so abused it took him six months to wag his tail.

Douglas still remains my dream dog. Assisting shelter animals is my passion, and Douglas is my invaluable helper. He was the inspiration for my children's book, *Broadway Barks.* He's also helping me to raise money for shelter animals and teaching children and adults the joy of adopting a pet from a shelter. He goes on personal appearances with me and loves getting applause. It's as if he'd been an actor in his last life.

Marina Poplavskaya

Singing in the children's chorus of the Bolshoi Theatre and debuting there in 2003, Russian soprano Marina Poplavskaya rose to prominence after standing in for Anna Netrebko in *Don Giovanni*, later performing in *Don Carlo* at the Royal Opera in London. Winner of the Maria Callas Grand Prix, she debuted at the Metropolitan Opera in 2007, and I met her through Gay Talese (page 202) at a Christmas party one year.

Since I was little girl, I was always surrounded by all sorts of different animals, all of which I loved taking care of. For example, we had a huge dog in our courtyard, and one day I discovered that she'd had puppies. For so many months those puppies were there, and I was around them, feeding, grooming, and talking to them.

I honestly believe that animals can talk, as they definitely understand any language. It doesn't matter if it's a pet or an animal in the wild, the line of communication is very strong between them and us. During my school years, I had an endless number of dogs, cats, hamsters, snakes, toads, birds, rabbits, turtles, and mice. We also had a couple of wonderful dogs that my grandfather kept in our village house. One, a small black terrier who loved singing, was named Chuka, and she really sang when my grandfather played his harmonica. The other two were big and not a particular breed, but they served well, doing their duty, keeping my grandpa company and protecting our grounds.

Marina Poplavskaya as a child with the courtyard dog's puppies

When I was seven, I was bringing home dozens of homeless dogs, to feed them at our apartment. Many times I gave them a nice, clean wash, using my mother's expensive rose oil and the best of her conditioners, so the dogs smelled just wonderful! Also I volunteered as a dog watcher/walker for most of my neighbors' pets. It felt so safe and fun when we shared our time together, communicating, playing, and learning from each other, just me and the dogs. These days, in my travels, always on the move, I do miss that blessed time, when I had my restless friends around.

Today I carry with me around the world a stuffed animal, a dog named Fufe. I adopted him from a basket where they were selling toys in aid of a local children's hospital and cancer center. They advertised that every toy purchased might prolong a child's life, which of course made me want to help. I always donate to children's charity hospitals and research centers in my travels.

But Fufe has even more meaning to me. It brings me back to my childhood and helps me to remember how it feels to be with a beloved pet, through memories of those very important moments. Today, on cold nights, Fufe is a warming pad for my throat and also my friend who knows my secrets and who is happy to listen. This toy dog has traveled all over the world with me.

Natalie Portman and Charlie with his trademark Gorbachev belly freckles

Natalie Portman

Animal rights and environmental activist Natalie Portman won the Academy Award, Golden Globe, BAFTA, SAG, and Independent Spirit awards for her lead role in Darren Aronofsky's *Black Swan*. Other notable film roles include *Closer, V for Vendetta,* the *Star Wars* prequel trilogy, and *Garden State.* When she decided she wanted to direct, she phoned Ben and asked if he would help her by acting in a short film. It was called *Grandma,* with that character played by Lauren Bacall. I came to the set one night and asked Natalie for her story, which she happily shared.

The saddest thing about eulogies—and there are many sad things about eulogies—is that the sentiments should have been expressed during the deceased's lifetime. Now that the person is gone, those remaining finally recognize how much the deceased impacted their lives, and regret ensues for all the unspoken gratitude and unexpressed love.

But with my dear departed dog, Charlie, there is none of that regret, because with dogs, of course, no words can convey love or appreciation. Only behavior can express love, and so the relationship doesn't leave anything unsaid. The whole relationship is unspoken. So Charlie, I will now let other people know how much I love you.

I met Charlie when he was between three and five years old, according to his teeth. He was a rescue. A friend from an organization called A Cause for Paws found him in a junkyard. When he arrived, he had bald patches where chunks of tar had been cut out of his fur, and he was severely underweight.

But whatever unknown horrors he had experienced before we met, he never acted out the resultant traumas for as long as I knew him. He was gentle to people—male and female, young and old—and to dogs and cats, especially cats. Charlie was particularly catlike himself. He curled his back elegantly, jumped well from high places, and licked his paws as if they were covered in milk. He loved to curl up fetally and felinely in the dog bed formed by my knees and stomach while I was lying on my side. He had brown freckles, Gorbachev-shaped, all over his belly, and he displayed them freely in exchange for a belly rub.

He also had razor-sharp intuition. I went through a particularly difficult breakup after having had Charlie for three years, and I was lying in bed, unable to motivate myself to get up. I was crying and feeling sorry for myself and thinking how I couldn't even see right—everything was blurry from the crying. Charlie started licking my tears, reminding me that I had forgotten the real man in my life. He saved me from being too inside my own head. I needed to get up to walk him and feed him, and it wasn't all about my silly broken heart.

Charlie passed away last summer while I was in London. My mother had been watching him for me, and had taken him for his annual teeth cleaning. The anesthesia was too much for him, and he decided to remain asleep. I have no words that I wish I'd said to him because he wouldn't have understood them anyway. This eulogy is more for him than for me: to appreciate how much can be felt and expressed without saying anything; to remember how he got me out of bed in the morning and made me feel loved more than anyone's words ever have; and to remember that it's my mission to find that wordless love in every moment and in all the tenderness around me.

Jane Powell and Charles Dickens

Jane Powell

I grew up in Germany, so it was Ben who told me about the young Jane Powell, who was wonderful in so many big MGM musicals like *Royal Wedding* and *Seven Brides for Seven Brothers*. She's still wonderful, and a delight to be with.

As a child I was a cat person, because my mother didn't like dogs. But ever since I was given one of Lassie's pups as a pet, both dogs and cats have been part of my life. Having been on the road for thirty years, traveling with one, sometimes three, children, and two or three dogs, I remember many happy, funny, sometimes even frightening times with my four-legged friends.

One special memory from more recent years involves my miniature poodle, Charles Dickens. He was an extraordinary dog who became a loving caregiver to my first poodle, December the First, when December went blind. Dickens loved my husband, Dick, and followed in his footsteps as he worked in the garden.

For the 1988 holiday celebrations, Dickens was chosen to be "master of cere-bonies" at June Havoc's annual Blessing of the Animals, a major annual outdoor celebration near our home in Connecticut. Dickens, like his Lhasa Apso stepsister, Suzie, was twenty at the time. I think they both lived so long because, for them, every day was a new adventure.

Dickens was thrilled to be chosen to lead the celebration. It was his first "Blessing." He wore a red coat that covered his receding fur and a Christmas boutonniere. My husband held him so that he could see and be seen. Dickens assumed that I would write and deliver his speech, since he was unaccustomed to public appearances and had lost the projection in his bark. I delivered his opening remarks to the assembly. They began:

"I am 140 years old and still living at home."

The crowd's reaction was enthusiastic, and I believe that Dickens, though he was quite deaf, heard them, acknowledging their applause with a wag of his frail tail. Obviously show business was in his blood.

That was Dickens's last personal appearance; it was a glorious Connecticut day, and a perfect finale for my darling master of cere-bonies.

Rex Reed

In 1979 I met Ben in Seoul, South Korea. He was making *Inchon* with Laurence Olivier and a lot of other interesting people, including great film critic and good buddy, Rex Reed, who also appeared in *Superman* and *Myra Breckenridge*, authored *Do You Sleep in the Nude?*, *People Are Crazy Here,* and *Valentines & Vitriol,* among other books, and now writes a column for the *New York Observer.*

When I was just a wee tyke in rompers, I had my first dog—a mutt named Jinky Boy. I don't know where the name came from, but I remember vividly this dog's obsession with chasing merrily after me, knocking me down, and ripping my diapers off—in the yard, the driveway, the street. I fell screaming, half-naked, until my mother came running to the rescue, waving a wooden spoon to drive away my pet.

By the time I was two, it was the same story. Instead of diapers, though, Jinky Boy went after my little briefs. Publicly I was a smart kid—saying my ABCs on the radio. Privately, with nothing on below the waist except my socks, I was the world's first two-year-old porn star.

I loved that mischievous dog. He accompanied me on my first day at school and waited outside to carry home my first-grade spelling book in his teeth.

Everybody loved Jinky Boy except my father, who remained unshaken in his firm belief that dogs shouldn't be allowed inside the house. Eventually, on rainy nights, he relented enough to allow my dog to escape from the elements and sleep on the back porch, but one foot over the threshold and inside the door was strictly off limits to anything with four legs, no matter how beloved.

Jinky Boy, showing unusual restraint, and Rex Reed

One thing my father did love was fishing. Oddly, he seemed anxious to take the dog with him for his outings on the rivers, lakes, and Louisiana swamps, but every time he yelled, "Come on, boy— let's go!" my faithful dog, who took after me, hid behind that pecan tree. The dog had no interest in sitting around in a boat while people tried to catch silly old fish. He preferred waiting for me after school, outside the ice cream parlor, in hopes that some careless child might drop a melting scoop of pistachio on the sidewalk.

One day, my father caught Jinky Boy off guard, scooped him up in his beefy arms, and dragged him off to the river to keep him company while he fished for trout. By the time he got home, his enthusiasm astounded my mother and me. He could scarcely contain his newfound praise for a pet he had always previously eyed with suspicion, or ignored entirely. What happened? It seems that while his back was turned to inspect his rod and reel, a poisonous cottonmouth snake had squirmed its way into his rowboat unannounced. Jinky Boy went berserk, barking ferocious alarm signals that you could hear halfway to Texas.

My father never would have seen this slithering reptile adversary if it hadn't been for my dog, who received a welcome-home dinner of steak tartare, green grapes (a secret favorite), and warm milk fit for a hero. After his meal, he curled up for a long snooze under the kitchen table on my father's suede hunting jacket from the Sears Roebuck catalog. It was the last time Jinky Boy ever spent the night in the garage or on the screened-in porch.

I've had other dogs since then, but Jinky Boy is the one I will never forget.

Marty Richards, his niece Casey Johnson, and Pip

Martin Richards

An old friend and a busy man, Marty Richards produced big Broadway musicals and big Hollywood movies. He won the Academy Award for *Chicago* and won Tony Awards for *Sweeney Todd, La Cage aux Folles, The Will Rogers Follies,* and *The Life.* He helped found Broadway Cares / Equity Fights AIDS, as well as the New York Center for Children, which cares for abused children and their families. He died in 2012, but before that he kindly made time to talk to me about another of his passions.

The dachshund is the best of all possible dogs. I've had four of them throughout my life, but the last was the one who got to me the most. Samson was a brown, short-haired mini, like Maxi, but even smaller. I used to wear him around my neck like a fur collar. He followed me everywhere but hated going out in the rain. He walked in it like a ballet dancer, his feet hardly touching the wet pavement. We sent him to three different training schools, but he never could graduate. Finally, we said, "What the hell; he's so small, what difference does it make?"

There was already an older dachshund in the house—Kate, named after Katharine Hepburn—and a Shih Tzu named for Warren Beatty. Well, Kate gave birth to three pups that we named Missy, Toby, and Sweeney, after the characters in *Sweeney Todd.* My wife, MaryLee, and I called them "shithunds."

Samson was only one year old when he took a shine to Missy, in particular, and they slowly but surely became lovers and acted like husband and wife. They never left each other's sight, and their affair went on for years. We were all very sad when, at the age of eleven, Missy went blind. But rather than brood and worry, Samson went to work. He became her seeing-eye dog, leading her through doors, across rooms, to her feeding bowl, and to her bed at night, where they slept together.

This went on for two years before Missy died. Samson, up to then showing the stamina of a dog half his age, began to weaken. I'm sure he had remained strong in order to care for the love of his life. I saw that he was faltering, and I knew he wouldn't be with me for long. So I remained near him, caressing and hugging him as often as possible. When he died, I thought I'd never stop crying. What a dog—I still miss him.

I'd decided never again to get a dog . . . but a few months later, Woody Johnson, a good friend, told me that his golden retriever had given birth to nine pups and asked if I'd like one. Well, I'd heard that the retriever was a very good companion, so I thought I'd take a look.

All nine little creatures were adorable, but my eyes kept going to the fattest and biggest of the brood. When I picked him up and he licked my face, my nose, and even my mouth, I was his. I told Woody he had a deal and headed home with my new bundle of joy. Our New York apartment was quite large, and there was also a country house made to order for a frisky dog. Every pooch in that litter wound up in a very fancy place to live. Woody Johnson and his wife, Sayle, knew only the rich and famous.

I named the dog Pip after the boy in *Great Expectations*. Well, the small dog became extra-big and beautiful. I was proud to walk with him, to show him off, and to stop and chat with people who paused to admire him.

As you know, golden retrievers are great water dogs. As soon as Pip saw the ocean, he made a mad dash for it, dived under the incoming waves, swam out, came back, and did it all over again. It was a pleasure to watch him. As a matter of fact, I think I enjoyed myself more with that dog than with most of the people I knew at the time. He had become a dear friend.

But at about the age of eight or nine, he started to slow down. I saw that he was developing a kind of limp. I took him to the vet, whose diagnosis was hip dysplasia, a condition that big dogs often develop.

Pip was great. He lived with that painful problem for five years. As it slowly worsened, I took him to the vet at least once a week. We tried everything, even acupuncture, but nothing worked. I decided to take him to the country, where there was a swimming pool that he loved. He spent most of the day swimming, which was painless for him. He dived into the water easily and swam happily, but getting him out was tough. I had to push and lift his backside until all of his paws reached dry land. It was hard work but a labor of love—and I think that swimming pool added at least two years to Pip's life.

When we were back in New York, he was having more and more trouble walking. Henry Kissinger lives in our building, and he had a big black Labrador who must have had similar problems. I saw him often with the dog, which was seated in an open red children's wagon. He pulled the animal through the lobby and out into the street for his morning walk. Henry's devotion to that creature impressed me. I thought I might try the same thing, but it was too late. Pip was no longer in control of his bowels or his urinary tract. When he went all over himself, he looked up at me, shamefaced, as though to apologize. It broke my heart.

I called the vet and told him what was going on, and he said that I wasn't doing Pip a favor. The dog was hanging on because of me. I hung up and watched Pip and his brave struggle to live. He was fighting for breath. Whenever he moved there was pain. I watched him for a long time before I could face the fact that I had to let him go.

It's the hardest decision I've ever made.

Mickey Rourke

Giving up boxing to become an actor, Mickey Rourke first came to fame in films such as *9½ Weeks, Diner,* and the critically praised *Barfly.* Ben did a picture called *13* with Rourke, who was fresh off the enormous success of *The Wrestler,* for which he won a Golden Globe and thanked his dogs in his acceptance speech. I had read that Mickey loved dogs, so I gave Ben a tape recorder and asked him to get me a story.

I lived with six dogs—four Chihuahuas, a pug, and a Samoyed, which is like a mini Eskimo. One of my Chihuahuas is named Loki. Her father was Beau Jack, whom I named after a great fighter from the 1940s. Her mother was Angel. She had two brothers and a sister, Chocolate, Romy, and Monkey. Now seventeen years old, Loki is the last of that litter. Before I got the new dogs, I used to take her everywhere. I never left her alone. Even when I worked in England, I had a friend fly to Paris and drive her through to London. Once I did leave her for a few days, and she had a stroke. That happens to dogs sometimes—old dog syndrome, it's called.

I don't trust people who don't like dogs. A friend was sitting on my couch once. My dog jumped onto it to keep him company, and he pushed the dog away. I didn't like the look in his eyes when he did that, and I lost respect for him. How can you not love dogs? I couldn't live without them.

In the '90s, I went through a bad period. Work wasn't coming, money was disappearing, and the woman I was crazy about left

Mickey Rourke and Loki

me. I really loved that girl, and I wanted her back. I knew I needed help, a miracle, maybe, so I decided I'd go to Lourdes. But I had a dog then, too, Loki's father, Beau Jack. Beau was fifteen years old and needed care. Thank God I still had a few friends left; one of them volunteered to stay at my place while I made the trip.

The line to reach the grotto was long, made up of people of all ages, walking, in wheelchairs, on crutches, some even carried on stretchers. I was ashamed to be there. Suddenly, my problems didn't seem very important. But I finally arrived at the statue of Mary, knelt down, closed my eyes, and prayed. I asked for forgiveness.

My girlfriend did come back, but every promise I'd made to her I broke. I was hopeless. I was letting everything slip away. There were no movies, no money, no woman. The entourage left, and I sat down in my closet, curled up, and didn't move. I even slept in there. I didn't leave the house for four or five months—until one day I came to a decision. I was going to do some bad shit, but I looked up, and there was Beau Jack, staring not at me but *through* me. It was like he was saying, *You ain't going nowhere. Who's going to take care of me?*

The most important thing about having a dog and loving a dog is that you have to be responsible, and you have to communicate with your animal. He has to know how much he means to you. Sometimes, when a man is alone, that's all he's got: his dog. That could mean the world to you.

It took a dog to save my life. That's why I tell people: If you lose your dog, get another one right away. Go down to the pound and rescue one of those loving, thankful guys. You know, if they asked me whom I'd rather be with on a desert island, a woman or a dog, well . . . let me think about that.

Gena Rowlands, Robert Forrest, and Phoebe

Gena Rowlands

Two-time Golden Globe winner and dear friend Gena Rowlands made her Broadway debut in *The Seven Year Itch*. After appearing on the soap opera *Peyton Place,* she went on to make movies such as *Gloria, Minnie and Moskowitz,* and *A Woman Under the Influence.* Twice nominated for Academy Awards, she was married to John Cassavetes until his death in 1989. Gena had been a good friend of Ben before I met him, and they starred in several films together, including *Hysterical Blindness*—which won her a third Emmy—so I've known her now for more than three decades. Gena spent most of her life without dogs because of her asthma, and she never thought she'd have one.

As a child, I often visited friends who had dogs, and I always came home wheezing, so I was resigned to never being able to own a dog. I was happy just to look at them, and looking was all I did for many years. But when my kids got older, they started wanting a dog, like everybody's kids, and I said, "I can't; I just can't do it. I'm sorry. No!" But they kept at it.

We had a friend who showed up suspiciously often with a German shepherd—well, half German shepherd, half Lab. John loved shepherds because he'd had them as a boy. So I finally thought that they could have their dog, and I would just stay away from him. Well, of course, as fate had it, I just fell in love with that dog, and he, Cosmo, followed me everywhere. The kids were out doing their own thing, and I realized nobody was really taking care of him, so I took care of Cosmo. I thought it would be okay since he was short-haired, but apparently that wasn't the problem.

This was the worst allergy dog ever. I was stuffed up all the time. Still, I couldn't wait for everyone else to leave the house in those days so I could be alone with Cosmo. We were really friends.

Cosmo was darling with the kids—he let them ride on him, and they put hats and boots on him, things like that. I have a great picture of Cosmo taken while I was doing a publicity shoot at the house. The minute that dog saw a camera, he ran right over and sat there in front of it. He died in the 1980s, a few years before John. I knew then that as much as I loved Cosmo, I would never have another dog, and I was okay with that.

Then, some twenty years after Cosmo, one of my daughters mentioned that she had seen this new breed from Australia on *Good Morning, America* that wasn't supposed to cause allergies. She said it was called a Labradoodle—half Labrador and half poodle.

Months later, when Christmas came around, we received a mysterious phone call from the kids telling us to pick up our present at a specified time at the Continental Airlines freight desk at LAX. It was a plot, and they were all in on it.

Armed with just a flight number and an arrival time, Robert, my husband, and I drove to the airport. During the drive I told Bob that if it was a dog, it was definitely going back. "No way would the kids send us a dog," he said. "They know you're allergic. Between your asthma and our travel schedule, I think they would send us an iguana before they sent us a dog."

Well, we arrived at LAX, and when the little crate was delivered to us, Bob looked down immediately and said, "Damn! It's a dog!"

"Oh God, it's a dog!" I echoed.

When the crate opened, out came this little blonde puppy, and I melted right away. The pooch was irresistible. I wanted to take a closer look, and when I brought her nearer to my face, she threw her little paws around my neck and kind of plastered herself against me. That was it. I knew I was a goner.

However, what I thought would be a small dog that we could easily travel with eventually turned out to weigh fifty-five pounds—a lot bigger than we had bargained for. Nonetheless, she's our dream dog.

Phoebe is six years old now, and I spend an awful lot of time with her. Every day we go for walks, whether in Palm Springs around the golf course or in LA, up in the Hollywood Hills. Phoebe keeps me on my toes, and, wonder of wonders, I've never sneezed or wheezed, not even once.

Twombly mugging for a treat

Ralph Rucci

Fashion designer Ralph Rucci and I met years ago when we were sitting next to each other at a gala and he complimented the Oscar de la Renta gown that I was wearing—and of course our conversation soon turned to our mutual love of dogs. Rucci learned his craft at the hem of Halston and one of Balenciaga's patternmakers, and his work now hangs in museum collections across the globe. In 2008 Martha Stewart narrated a profile of him that aired on the Sundance Channel, and in recent years he has accrued an impressive number of distinctions, including: the Artistry of Fashion Award from the Couture Council of The Museum at FIT, the Fashion Design Award of the Cooper-Hewitt National Design Museum, the Icon Award from Pratt Institute, and the André Leon Talley Lifetime Achievement Award from the Savannah College of Art and Design. Among others, Rucci has taken inspiration for his work from Elsa Peretti and, as you'll see, painter Cy Twombly.

The phone rang one afternoon, and I heard the excited shouts of my friend: "Get here immediately. Right now. You must see this bulldog puppy." I was working; it was hard to leave, and I said as much. Ninety seconds later, a text message arrived with a photo. I was out the door and in a taxi moments later on my way uptown.

I may have gasped when I saw him because I had never before seen anything that looked quite like him. He had a completely white head with one black ear, and his pudgy body was completely black and his paws brown. The colors didn't change in grades but, rather, abruptly—where the white ended the black immediately began so that he seemed to be wearing a coat. Of course, I wanted him immediately but hesitated because the asking price was quite high. The next day, I was off to Paris for work and a bit of holiday, but I couldn't get the little bulldog out of my head. Upon arrival in Paris, I phoned the pet shop and told them that I had to have him. In fact, I had already named him: Twombly.

I picked him up several days later and twenty-four hours after that noted that his continually clamped-shut eyes were oozing pus. I took him straight away to our beloved veterinarian, Barbara Kalvig. After several days' worth of examinations and analyses, we determined that his tear sacs were destroyed and, since his eyes couldn't be lubricated, they had filled with infection. It was later confirmed that the cause of this enormous problem was an operation he underwent at the pet shop from which he was purchased. Apparently he was born with "cherry eyes," and to render him more marketable they removed his "cherries." In doing so, they also destroyed his tear sacs. Getting them to come clean required at least five days of endless probing by Dr. Kalvig.

Various forms of treatment were decided upon, and he went through several operations—not to correct the problem, which really couldn't be corrected—but to circumvent it. After many exercises in trial and error, countless doctor visits and medications, and three surgical procedures, he gradually improved, his eyes almost completely healthy.

Now, almost seven years later, Twombly lives with me on the Upper East Side in a wonderful air-conditioned apartment with a large terrace and is looked after all day by a very loving and always attentive sitter/housekeeper. Whenever he needs to travel around the city, he does so in a hired car and consequently thinks that every Lincoln sedan he sees belongs to him. His demeanor is more gentle, kind, and sweet than that of most people, and he is loved so totally by my staff that when he comes into the office there is literally a welcoming committee awaiting him behind closed elevator doors. The hugging, kissing, loving, and playing never end until he falls asleep under one of the patternmaker's tables.

He has been on *The Martha Stewart Show* twice and is always very well behaved on camera. He has been the subject of a blog on Vogue.com and has been photographed for no fewer than five books. He is treated with great love and care by everyone who knows him, and his behavior reflects that love and care in every way. In truth, you cannot walk him around the block without being stopped by half a dozen people each time who wish to photograph and play with him. He is my beloved little son who has enriched my life—and the lives of everyone who knows him—immeasurably and profoundly.

Frieda Number Two giving Mark Ruffalo a kiss

Mark Ruffalo

Oscar-nominated for his role in *The Kids Are All Right*, Mark Ruffalo has also appeared in Marvel's *The Avengers*, *Eternal Sunshine of the Spotless Mind*, *Zodiac*, and *Shutter Island*. His directorial debut, *Sympathy for Delicious*, won the Special Jury Prize at Sundance. In 2006, Ben took part in a splendid revival of Clifford Odets's *Awake and Sing!* in New York, for which Mark was nominated for a Tony. He later came to our hotel on the beach in Santa Monica, where we shared Mexican food, frozen margaritas, and a lot of laughs. But it was no free lunch; I made him work for it.

I was living in LA and looking for work as an actor. I had almost no money, so I split the rent with another struggling actor on a sort of little house in West LA—more like a shack, really.

It was Thanksgiving, and an actress friend invited us to her house for dinner, where there'd be a lot of people we knew. I was looking forward to it. It was about one p.m. when we left our house, but when we opened the door, lying on our little porch was a dog, all straggly and dirty. She had what looked like a lamp cord around her neck, which she'd broken free of. The dog looked up but didn't move. She looked unhappy, and we figured she'd been abused and abandoned.

I got some scissors and got that cord off of her. There was dried blood all around her neck. She obviously had fought like hell to free herself. I filled a pot with cold water and placed it nearby. Then I brought her some meat loaf from the night before, and we left. I felt bad for that animal.

The wine at the feast was that cheap Gallo red, and I drank it happily, but when we left I was a little high, so my friend Charlie drove. We parked in front of our house and saw that the dog was still there. She was waiting for us. I think we both hoped she would be, and knew right away that we were going to keep her. We took her to the vet, who gave her shots and cleaned her up. From a dirty, wretched creature, she became beautiful. I don't understand how people can take a gentle, loving life and treat it with such cruelty.

We named her Frieda; I don't remember why. In time, she became my dog. I took her everywhere—on auditions, to meetings, to parties—and at one of those gatherings I met a very attractive girl with a great body. We liked each other very much, so she took me and Frieda to her place. It was like a studio apartment—you know, where everything is in one space. Well, when it got to the moment of truth, she said that Frieda had to wait outside. I guess she didn't want her jumping into bed with us. She said that I could tie her to a nearby post, and she'd be safe. Well, I had to think fast. Should I leave now or pretend to go along? I was very horny, so I double-crossed her, rushing my pleasure and getting out of there in ten minutes. Frieda was very happy to see me, and I felt guilty that I'd left her, and very bad about leaving that girl. It was a sacrifice, believe me. What a night it could have been.

I started getting more work. In time, I got my own pad and took Frieda with me. For seven years, she was my constant companion, and then I lost her. A car ran her over. It took me a long time to get over it. I never even thought about getting another dog again. The loss was too painful.

Years later, after I married and my wife was eight months pregnant, she called me and told me she'd bought a little puppy.

"What? Are you crazy?" I said. "You're going to have a baby and raise a dog at the same time?"

"I had to see what it's like to be a mother."

I laughed, she laughed, and we had ourselves a dog—a Belgian breed that's hard to spell: Schipperke, a Belgian barge dog. It was all black and looked like a little fox. They say it was among the first dogs ever to wear a collar. The skipper of the barge would clip his key to the dog's collar, knowing it was so loyal that it would never allow anyone else to come near it. They're water dogs, known to rescue many a drunken barge hand who fell into the drink. They're very protective animals, and, like cats, they like to climb things.

When our son was about a year and a half old, we bought a place in upstate New York with a pond and willow trees—very pretty. Frieda Number Two was the same age as the baby, but she weighed about twenty-five pounds by then, and she lay under our son's bassinet, protecting him. She loved him.

One day, we were outside, the baby sitting on a blanket playing with his toys, Frieda doing her thing, and I was on the phone. It was a business call and dealt with a difficult issue, so I strolled away so as not to yell in front of the baby. When I'd finished, I turned and saw that my little son was waddling as fast as he could toward the pond and Frieda was on his heels. I could have run and picked him up, but before I could make my move, Frieda had already dashed in front of him, reared up, pushed against his chest with her paws, and knocked him on his fanny. She knew danger when she saw it. All she thought about was saving the baby. What a dog. She's still with us and will be forever, I hope.

COURTESY OF PRINCESS CLAUDIA RUSPOLI

*Princess Ruspoli, Lupetta, Nettuno, Sweetie, and
Matteo in the gardens of Castello Ruspoli*

Princess Claudia Ruspoli

Ben was doing a film in Rome and we were staying at the Majestic Hotel, which we had last visited years earlier to have drinks and laughs with Frank Sinatra and his wife, Barbara. Tired when we arrived, we decided to have dinner in the hotel dining room. In the restaurant, seated across from us, was Princess Claudia Ruspoli, whom I hadn't seen in some time. She hails from one of the oldest aristocratic families in Italy. They can trace their roots back to the time of Charlemagne, and in 1721 Pope Benedict XIII raised the family to their princely rank. More recently Claudia restored the gardens of Castello Ruspoli, the family seat, forty miles north of Rome. I'd heard she loved dogs, so I was anxious to talk to her. We met again the next day, over lunch in the Villa Borghese, and this is what she told me.

As a child I had cats, but then as a teenager I started to pick up abandoned or wounded dogs from the street. Some were so afraid that they bit me. I had to get anti-rabies injections in my tummy. When the dogs were calm and cured, I found homes for them among my friends. This continued into my twenties, but the time finally came when I felt I had to travel. I was something of a gypsy in those days.

My father gave me one of the family castles, the one just outside Viterbo in the Lazio region. I have lived there for the last fifteen years. It was in 1996, I think, that my gardener found a stray dog. It seems she was living on my property, summer and winter.

She was apricot in color and had the face of a wolf—beautiful. I fell in love immediately, so I decided to give her a home. I was all by myself in that castle; the only person I saw was the gardener, and it was lonely. Having a playful young dog as company was a joy.

She was female, and she was pretty, so the playboys in the neighborhood, one or two at a time, showed up, and soon she was pregnant. She had seven puppies, and I didn't know what to do. I gave four puppies to friends and kept three for myself. The mamma's name is Lupetta, and the kids are Nettuno, Sweetie, and Matteo. Sweetie is the only girl. The mother and the three children look like a mixture of wolf and husky. They are gorgeous. I never trained them—they trained themselves. When they were small, I spent at least two hours a day picking up their poo.

One night, I looked out my bedroom window and saw a lovely white long-haired dog standing under a lamppost. I watched that dog for three nights. It was obviously abandoned, which happens often in my area. On the fourth night, I went out with water and food. She was stunning, a mixture of hunting dog and show dog. Her white fur was spotless, and her eyes sparkled. She was afraid, but very slowly she came to me. What can I say? She became my dog, and I called her Bedu.

But I had a problem. How would I introduce her to Lupetta and her kids? They would be very jealous. I was afraid they might even kill her. So I kept them separated. She had her own section of the castle to sleep in and play in. When I went on trips all over Europe by car, I took Bedu with me.

While I was driving to Milan, my gardener phoned me. Lupetta, fourteen, had suffered a stroke. I got back to the castle as fast as I could. The vet had already been there. The medication helped her to walk more straight. Now she never leaves my side. Age had caught up with her, and I had to decide what to do. Now the gardener looks after Bedu so that Lupetta can be with me night and day. She sleeps in my bed while her children sleep nearby. She needs all the love she can get, and I am going to give it to her.

I'm a loner. Oh, here and there I've had boyfriends for short periods in my life. I wasn't lucky with men. I never got married, so I don't have children. Now, if I could, I would live with a zoo full of animals, all kinds—goats, pigs, cows, sheep, chicken, cats, and, of course, dogs. Whatever the city, if there is a park, I run with dogs. I climb hills with them. I play and roll on the ground with them. They give me enormous energy.

May Andersen (8½ months pregnant), Julian Schnabel, and Buddy

Julian Schnabel

First gaining widespread acclaim for his broken ceramic plate paintings, Julian Schnabel became a major figure in Neo-Expressionism. Later turning to film, he directed the critically acclaimed *Basquiat*, *Before Night Falls,* and *The Diving Bell and the Butterfly*, the last of which earned him an Oscar nomination and best director awards from the Cannes Film Festival, the Golden Globes, and the Independent Spirit Awards. Having met him through Frank Gehry (page 44), Ben was a fan and friend since Julian was known only as a painter. I will forever think of him with a warm heart because in Ben's final days, Julian came to the hospice and read him the entire script for a picture that he wanted Ben to do along with Johnny Depp, giving him a few last days of joy.

My name is now Buddy. It used to be Elvis. That's not because I was Elvis—you know, the singer—but because I may be part hound. Get the joke? But they didn't really know what I was. I was wondering if I should write this in first person, or first dog, so to speak, because I'd like to tell you my version of the events leading up to my adoption by my new family.

I was standing outside the Animal Rescue Foundation (ARF) Dog Refugee Camp with a young handler when the most beautiful girl I'd ever seen took notice of me and smiled the biggest, most gigantic, friendly smile at me as the wind caught her hair and blew her through the glass doors of the animal rescue center, where I was biding my time. With her she had—how can I say it . . . a big, friendly teddy bear of a person who also had a warm smile and deep raisin eyes. I wondered if I would ever see them again. Other families had come to look at me, and I was just hoping for some kindness and love.

I had been shipped around quite a bit from kill shelter to kill shelter in North Carolina and had seen some things. Some dogs get lucky; some just get dealt a bad hand. At six months, I was almost too tall to be cute, but not to them. When I got called into the office, I was pleasantly surprised to see them waiting for me. I felt an instant connection, but then after fifteen minutes they left. I felt despair and a deep sense of loss.

The next day came with regularity and a tinge of sadness. I had dreamt of them and was still thinking of what life could be like with them, when a family of five—three children, two boys and a girl, all about four feet tall, and their parents—corralled me for a walk. As we walked, they touched me, and the littler boy hugged me as their mother told them in a militant voice how they would have to clean up after me.

All of a sudden a dog handler approached the father and whispered something to him and then went inside to the office. The father seemed serious and annoyed. After ten minutes, I was also brought in, where I found the pretty girl and the man from the day before. The girl's face was red and distressed as she held me and rubbed my neck with her gentle hands. It happened that the girl, whose name is May, had signed an application to adopt me the day before, but the workers at the rescue center had misplaced her application.

The father of the children came in to state his case: He didn't really care, but his children were in love with me, and how could he break the news to them that they had to select another dog? Even though they had found the papers and May was in the right, she was torn, thinking that, if they didn't get me, two dogs would end up losing a home. I have never seen such a sad face on a human before. The father of the family of five insisted that it would crush his children.

I thought all was lost and May was going to give in to her gentleness when all of a sudden the man with the raisin eyes blurted out: "What about *my* child?" pointing at May. In that moment, the sadness got lost in the confusion of that bold statement. That said everything. Discussion closed. The man with the raisin eyes wasn't May's father, but he became mine, and May is my mom. What they don't know is that before I was Buddy the dog I was Johnny Carson, and being Buddy the dog isn't so bad.

Tess Serranti

An international business consultant for Patton Boggs, one of the top twenty international law firms, Tess Serranti is a high-powered businesswoman whom I met through her uncle, a journalist for *Corriere della Sera,* one of Italy's oldest and most respected newspapers. She also advises the government of Ghana about energy and privatization, but what continues to amaze me is the size of her heart. She found her big mutt Banana on the streets in Ghana, and Faustino, on the streets of Italy. Both are too big to travel, so they now stay mostly at her home in New Jersey with their many little brothers and sisters. Amazingly, at night, she sleeps completely surrounded by all of them! While Tess has many stories to share, my favorite is how she met the first of her many Chihuahuas.

Tess Serranti surrounded by some of her many Chihuahuas

About ten years ago, I flew to New York from London to attend a black-tie gala honoring the president of Ghana at the Plaza Hotel. When I got to my hotel to prepare for the evening, I cleaned up, did my hair and makeup, slipped into a champagne-and-black Valentino gown, and, while zipping up the back of the dress, broke one of my fingernails. Luckily, I was dressed early enough to wander the streets and look for someone to repair the nail. I slipped into a raincoat that covered only the top half of my gown and walked up and down Madison Avenue, but none of the manicure salons I could find were open. So I headed to Lexington Avenue and found a place above a flower shop. They fixed the nail in no time, and I headed back to my hotel. But, passing the American Kennels store, I saw something, stopped in my tracks, and went back to the window in which a sign read PUPPY——ON SALE——HALF PRICE.

"Why half price?" I asked inside the store. "What's wrong with her?"

"Oh, nothing's wrong with her."

"How old?"

"Seven months. That's the reason she's on sale. We've had her a while. She's a great dog, but nobody seems to want her."

Hearing that was all it took. "I want her. She's mine."

The moment I said that, the puppy looked up at me as though she knew somebody finally wanted her.

I left the store with my new little Chihuahua and rushed back to the hotel to finish preparing for the evening. I couldn't decide whether to take her to the party or leave her in the room. But the

More Chihuahuas!

puppy decided for me. She gave me a melancholy look as if to say, *Please take me with you!* So I did. The little thing fit perfectly in my black satin pouch, which I figured I could strap over my shoulder without anyone noticing I was carrying a dog.

The plan was working perfectly until the guest of honor, the president of Ghana, a tall, handsome man named Jerry John Rawlings, made his entrance with full presidential fanfare. The little puppy popped her head out of the pouch for a better view. The president stopped immediately in front of me, and, looking at the little animal, said, "And what's your name?"

"Isabella," I said, naming the dog on the spot.

"Isabella? And where is Ferdinando?"

"I haven't gotten him yet," I answered.

The president looked at me and said, "You must. A pretty girl should not be alone for too long."

"No, she shouldn't," I said, and oddly found myself blushing.

That encounter began a friendship that lasts to this day, and with that quick stop at the American Kennels store, I began a whole new family. Within a month, Isabella got her Ferdinando, and we spent the rest of the year traveling the world as a threesome. Since then, my little family has grown and grown. I've added a donkey, a cat, two rabbits, ten chickens, and fourteen more Chihuahuas—a regular zoo. Who knows what will be next?

Omar Sharif

Omar Sharif

Ben and I were in Paris on our way to the south of France. Our hotel was near the Champs-Élysées, so we decided to have dinner at Fouquet's, where we'd had many good times in the past. When we walked in, seated at the table near the entrance was Omar Sharif, whom we hadn't seen in almost twenty-five years. He demanded we join him and his companion for dinner. Of course it wasn't long before I asked if he had a dog.

In 1969, I made a movie called *Comes a Pale Horseman* and spent more than five months in Afghanistan, which at that time was still a monarchy. I got to know the king, and he took a liking to me. He and his guards visited the set on a very, very hot day, and the palace invited me to dinner with him and his family quite a few times. His dogs always accompanied him—two of the most beautiful gold-and-white Afghans I'd ever seen. During every dinner, they placed themselves near his chair and lay there until the meal ended. They loved their king; they were protecting him.

When the movie wrapped in Afghanistan, I had two weeks off before finishing the shoot in Spain. That gave me a chance to go home to Paris. Before heading to the airport, I went to the palace to say farewell. The king embraced me and wished me Godspeed. I thanked him for his kindness and generosity and vowed that the time would come when I'd see him again.

I was the only person sitting in top class. The other passengers had boarded, but more than an hour went by, and we still hadn't taken off. Then two men walked into the cabin, one holding a big dog on a leash. It was an Afghan, as beautiful as those I'd seen at the palace. The other man smiled and said that I would have no problems—that everything was in order. He then handed me veterinarian papers and enough dried food for at least a month. He told me that the dog would enjoy it more if I mixed it with chicken, lamb, or beef, and then handed me a note from the king, which read in Arabic: "His name is Bazo; he's a one-year-old. Be good to him, and he will repay you a hundredfold. God bless you both."

Bazo means "eagle" in Arabic, so I looked down at this dog and said, "Can you fly?"

He looked up at me, cocked his head, and wagged his tail. He had beautiful dark shiny eyes. *But what am I going to do with a dog?* I asked myself. The only experience I ever had with one was years before when I had lived in Egypt while married to a famous actress. After the wedding, we had a weeklong celebration cruising the Nile. But she wasn't alone; a small, mean, white dog came with her. From the beginning I didn't like the dog, and the dog hated me. The bitch was always nipping at my heels.

When the honeymoon ended and we settled into married life, the little sucker started sleeping in our bed right between us. She actually growled when I moved close to my wife, and once she even nipped at my private parts. So we put her in the next room, but she cried and barked and scratched at the door until we couldn't stand it any longer. My wife brought her back to our bed, making those goo-goo sounds that I never could stand. But what finally broke the camel's back was finding my brand-new Gucci loafers chewed up and mangled.

"You see, she has good taste," my wife said, giggling.

I asked why the dog didn't chew on her expensive clothes, and she answered that she was nice to the dog and I was not.

I told her, in no uncertain terms, "I don't like her. Why should I be nice to her?"

That's the way it went until the marriage ended, and I walked away—wearing Gucci loafers, by the way.

The flight from Kabul to Paris is long, so Bazo and I got to know each other. While I drank champagne, he drank his water. When it was time for dinner, I ordered a chicken, half of which I mixed with his dried food. We dined together, you might say. Then I sat him in the seat next to mine, and he licked my face as if to say thank you. That was it. I knew I had myself a dog.

I got Bazo a beautiful new red leather collar and leash. I wore my panama hat, a present when I finished *Lawrence of Arabia*, and we drove around Paris in my convertible Rolls-Royce. He sat up front with me, and we got a lot of attention. We drove along the Champs-Élysées into the Bois de Boulogne, where we hopped out of the car and Bazo and I strolled the boulevards. I sometimes dropped the leash to see what he would do, but he never left my side.

The women loved him, drawn to him even before they recognized me. He was a magnet. Any pretty lady who chose to join us sat in the backseat of the Rolls with Bazo next to her. He liked that a lot. He loved women. I've been accused of being a womanizer, but Bazo was worse. I took him everywhere. I hated to put him in the belly of a plane, but I wanted him with me. When I made a movie, he went on location with me. I took him to my home in Cairo, and even to the USA.

Bazo died when he was only seven years old, which broke my heart. He had become everything to me. He understood everything I said in five languages. I had no better friend and no better companion.

Liz Smith with two of the Dachsmith Love Kennels dachshunds

Liz Smith

The Grand Dame of Dish, Liz Smith has been a columnist since 1950. She is known for her signature gossip column that ran for over thirty years and continues to write for the *Huffington Post*. In the early 1960s, she became entertainment editor for *Cosmopolitan* under Helen Gurley Brown, and she won an Emmy in 1985 for her reporting on *Live at Five*. Her memoir, *Natural Blonde*, published in 2000, was a *New York Times* bestseller. We have known and liked her for many years—and not just because she loves dachshunds!

I was with my friend, the archaeologist Iris Love, who is a big dachshund fancier. We went over to New Jersey to see some puppies that a smooth-haired dachshund breeder was going to offer as soon as they emerged. We got there, looked at the bloated, gasping, about-to-be mother, and admired some other doxies who were barking and frisking about. The breeder, whom I shall call Kay, sat down in the middle of the floor to show us just how wonderful her dogs were.

Dachshunds being dachshunds, and quite jealous of their owners, Kay was soon awash in a snarl of dachshunds, and some of them got mad and started fighting. I didn't know then (but do now) that a dachshund fight is not something to be in the middle of, and before Kay could fight them off, separate them, and bring order, she was severely bitten and bleeding. *Well,* I said to myself, *if this is the dachshund world, I don't want any part of it.*

Iris, who heroically had been separating dogs with big glasses of thrown water, said she had better take Kay to the hospital. I agreed; she had to go. So they trundled off, and there I was in New Jersey, trapped in a house with a bitch about to give birth and other dachshunds now penned up or safely asleep.

Sure enough, the puppies decided to make their debut. I was desperate, like Butterfly McQueen in *Gone with the Wind*. I didn't know nothin' 'bout birthin' puppies. But nature has its own timetable, and the babies started coming. Soon the mother dragged herself under the bed, and I couldn't get her out, or help her. (I confess I didn't try very hard; I had just witnessed a dogfight, after all.)

When Iris and the freshly bandaged Kay finally returned from the hospital, there were several more little black-and-tan dachshunds in the world, but in my abandoned hysteria I had begun to fancy one in particular. Iris bought her for me after naming her Nike, the goddess of victory. (All Iris Love dogs have heroic Greek names!) Nike's nickname became "Liz the Lionhearted."

That's how I fell in love. Alas, I was often separated from Nike/Liz because she came from a line of champions and was frequently off touring and winning prizes all over America. I will spare you her credits, but Nike lived a long, happy, productive life, producing more champions and helping Iris and me create the Dachsmith Love Kennels in Vermont. It produces champs to this day.

I don't think I have ever been properly in love since, and when I see Nike, the Winged Victory, at the top of the stairs in the Louvre, I always salute and include my own remembered Nike.

Dara Sowell

One Sunday afternoon, while walking with Maxi in Central Park, I was crossing the bicycle trail and was almost run over by an attractive young woman, who I later learned was a model. She was dressed in white and riding a red bicycle. She stopped and asked if I was all right. Before I could answer, Maxi started barking and jumping up toward the basket hanging from the handlebars. At which, the head of a darling white Maltese popped out of the basket and barked back at Maxi. He was very brave, sitting high up on his perch.

"What's her name?" I asked.

"Charmin," she said.

"Excuse me?"

"Charmin, like the toilet paper."

I laughed, and we moved toward a bench to chat.

I was living and working in Miami. My fiancé, a real macho man, came home one day with this gorgeous little white Maltese dog. He couldn't find one he liked in a store or a shelter, so he'd searched out a breeder. What a guy.

But then we broke up, and I moved back to New York with my bundle of fur. I met another man here, and after we'd known each other for a month or two, he invited me to go back to Miami and spend a weekend at the romantic Delano Hotel. I liked him a lot, so I said yes. We had a problem, though; dogs weren't permitted at

Dara Sowell and Charmin

the Delano. But he talked to people, spread some money around, and Charmin was allowed to stay with us.

Restaurants, on the other hand, were a strict no. I had never left the dog alone anywhere, so we decided that she should stay in the car where the attendant would keep an eye on her. I rolled the windows down a little for Charmin to have enough air, and as I got out of the car I asked my new amour to lock the doors.

The restaurant was fancy but not overdone. We had delicious food and a lot of laughs. I think we were singing as we approached the car—but I heard no barking, no noise of any kind. That's because there was no dog; only her leash and collar remained on the backseat. My legs began to shake. I think I went into shock. I was a wreck. The poor guy began to defend himself, insisting that he'd locked the car, but clearly he hadn't.

We begged the parking attendant to think hard. Did anything out of the ordinary happen that night? Suddenly he remembered that four Latino boys had walked through the area at about ten p.m. I started to panic. What if they had hurt my little girl, abused her, thrown her around like a football? But the attendant wasn't through yet. He said he'd become suspicious, so he had memorized the first three numbers of the boys' license plate.

We took that information back to the hotel, but it was all we had. I was crying the whole night. No sleep. Forget about romance. I watched the clock. I couldn't wait for eight a.m. so we could go to the police station.

The sergeant at the desk was a dog lover and took my case seriously. He became my pal. I gave him the first three digits of the license and a picture of Charmin. I had posters made up with Charmin's picture and the announcement of a reward. I pasted them all over South and North Miami for three days.

Time was passing, but I wouldn't give up, I wouldn't go back to New York without my little girl. So I phoned my ex-fiancé, who had given me the dog. He was well connected in Miami and promised to help. He'd seen the poster, so he already knew the story. I hoped he would use his clout to help me. The police did what they could, but they had so many other cases to handle that mine was suspended.

I contacted the local TV stations and got a lot of turndowns until an important station in South Miami showed interest. They happened to be preparing a show called *Missing,* and after I told them the facts, the interviewer said that he wanted me to tell my story on the air.

"Oh no, I can't possibly be on TV. I haven't slept for days. I'm exhausted, I look horrible."

"That's even better," said the interviewer. "We'll have you picked up at your hotel in thirty minutes."

I tried to get myself together because I was a mess. I couldn't believe that a news show wanted my story: "Girl Comes from New York with Her Cute Little Dog, and Look What Happens." They put up a big picture of Charmin, and on the bottom of the screen it said STOLEN. In a very short time, more than a hundred phone calls came in. Some people thought that they had seen my dog, and some volunteered to search for her. That these strangers wanted to help me was astonishing.

I waited, but nothing happened. I began to believe she was gone forever. I cried myself to sleep, and on one of those sad nights, a little past midnight, my phone rang. A man's voice asked if I would be at home for a while.

"Of course," I said. "Where would I go?"

"I'll see you soon," he said, hanging up.

In about twenty minutes, a very handsome guy was at my door, and in his arms was the greatest gift I'd ever gotten. Charmin reached out to me as he handed her over. I asked if they'd hurt my little darling, and he assured me that she'd been well taken care of, even groomed and perfumed. I was nuzzling and kissing my Charmin, but stopped to ask how he had found her.

"I'll tell you, lady," he said. "A guy wanted to surprise his girl with a special birthday present, but he had no money."

"So he took my dog?"

"Looks that way."

"Why is he giving her back?"

"I talked him into it."

"Oh, you know him?"

"No, but now he knows me."

Then he was gone. Some guy. I will always be grateful to him.

Elaine Stritch and Adelaide

Elaine Stritch

Ben and Elaine knew each other for half a century, which means she's been my friend for half that time. She's as much fun in life as she is onstage. Known for her work on Broadway, including Stephen Sondheim's *Company,* she famously understudied Ethel Merman in *Call Me Madam* while starring down the block in *Pal Joey.* She also played Trixie Norton in *The Honeymooners* pilot (before the character was rewritten). In more recent years, the three-time Emmy winner gained acclaim for her captivating one-woman shows. One day, before she decamped for Michigan, I met her at the Carlyle Hotel, where she lived. We had high tea, and she gave me this wonderful story.

In the sixties, in London, in rehearsal, in the West End, in Noel Coward's musical, in *Sail Away*, in the part of Mimi Paragon, world-weary cruise hostess on the Cunard Line, a long-haired dachshund came into my life. She was a gift (what an understatement that is) from Noel Coward. She was to play my dog in *Sail Away* on *and* off stage. Noel Coward named her Adlai after Adlai Stevenson, the fifth United States ambassador to the United Nations. I don't think Mr. Coward was in any way interested in, or paid the least bit of attention to, the fact that my little dachshund was female. So, quietly, off stage, I changed her name to Adelaide. Who knew? Who cared?

The curtain went up opening night, and a chorus of stewards sang out, "Hallelujah, thank the Lord, Mimi Paragon is onboard."

With that I handed my dachshund to the head steward with a vintage Coward line: "Wilson, darling, be an angel, and take Adlai to the tip top most deck and give him a tiny walk. He's been up since dawn and hasn't had a moment." Adlai Stevenson, front row center, fell about. His laughter rose above the already huge reaction from the sold-out house at the Savoy Theater.

This was only the beginning of an extremely eventful and, needless to say, dramatic life that lay ahead for me, God knows, and for this magical miracle long-haired dachshund. We were inseparable.

Back in New York several years later, I was asked to come back once again to the West End in London and open the highly successful Harold Prince–Stephen Sondheim musical *Company*. I was not about to be separated from Adelaide, and the laws were firm in those days in England regarding quarantine—six months, and that was that.

Quarantine for Adelaide? Out of the question! "Greater love hath no man" than he who is trying to smuggle a four-legged friend into London, England, in the sixties. OK, here it goes, now it can be told.

I found a piece of luggage at T. Anthony's on Park Avenue, a sort of Madison Avenue businessman's bag—you know, scripts, contracts, etc.—measuring twenty by twelve inches. It was perfect for a dachshund. My sales clerk unzipped the bag, and Adelaide immediately jumped in it. It cost a fortune. She loved it, and I will tell you why: It meant that she was going, too. Off to the airport. With no X-ray jazz in those days, I boarded the plane, Adelaide in tow, of course. Quiet as a mouse, thank you, Jesus!

I said, "No, thank you," to drinks of any kind, booze mainly, for fear I would tell the captain, the pilot, the co-pilot, the stewardess, and anyone in first class who would listen about my traveling companion. I am telling you, believe me, I was a wreck.

Never mind, I persevered. Mercifully, I fell asleep. Surprisingly, Adelaide did not. Apparently the three sleeping pills that we picked up from the vet on the way to the airport didn't work at all! Bless her heart, not a sound, onward and upward.

We arrived at Heathrow on time, sailed through Customs thanks to the two double brandies I finally asked the stewardess to bring me, telling her I was afraid of landings. I invited the Customs investigator and his wife, if he had one, to the opening night of *Company* at Her Majesty's Theatre and to the party afterward at the Savoy. You can believe this or not: They came *and* had pictures taken for the *Evening Standard* with me and my dachshund, who, I explained to this Customs officer and his wife, was the company's opening-night present to me and that she was born in England in a kennel in Dorchester. Now, the final payoff: Adelaide lived with me at the Savoy Hotel, making her entrances in and exits out of the hotel in the T. Anthony bag—of course.

How I loved and adored that little dachshund. She lived for nineteen and a half years and brought sheer joy into my life onstage and off. You might say the reason for my enormous success at Her Majesty's Theatre in Noel Coward's musical *Sail Away* in the West End of London in the sixties was in the bag.

Gay and Nan Talese with Barclay and Benchley

Gay Talese

Many consider renowned author and essayist Gay Talese the greatest nonfiction writer of our day. For *Esquire* he famously wrote "Frank Sinatra Has a Cold" and "The Silent Season of a Hero," about Joe DiMaggio, and his books—*Honor Thy Father, The Kingdom and the Power, Thy Neighbor's Wife,* and the more recent *Unto the Sons* and *A Writer's Life* among them—have all been successful. He is married to Nan Talese, publisher of the eponymous imprint in the Knopf Doubleday Publishing Group of Random House. Ben and I had dinner one night with Gay and Nan, and during the meal I asked, "Gay, do you like your dogs?"

"I'm not sure," he said. "Why?"

"Well, I'm doing another book, and guess what it's about?"

"Is it about your husband and what a dog he is?"

"No, Gay," I said, laughing. "It's about many dogs—even yours. Do you think you can write me something about them?"

"Of course. I will write tonight. I'm most inspired in the dark, and I won't sleep until I get it right. You'll find it with your *New York Times* in the morning."

Dear Elke,

I'm sorry I didn't get this to you with your *New York Times*, but I'm also trying to get working on a book already overdue.

You wanted dog comments, and I'm afraid that our dogs (two Australian terriers), Barclay and Benchley, are really Nan's and not mine. One dog is about seven and the other about four. They are males, cousins, and probably homosexual, though they have lost interest in sex, it seems. Perhaps this is because both dogs need variety (like former governor Spitzer), and, since they're stuck with each other all day and all night, they've become asexual dogs, paying interest in nothing more than their thrice-daily feedings, for which they arrogantly bark at precisely 9:00 a.m., 3:15 p.m., and 7:45 p.m. Nan feeds them promptly when they bark. She always looks at her watch and is amazed at how the dogs can tell time.

The dogs were acquired as puppies. Before they came, we had other Australian terriers. There is nothing special about them except that they're spoiled, self-indulgent, and they can tell time.

Nan walks them when we're in Connecticut, but when we're home in New York—and Nan is in the office—we have professional dog walkers come by two times a day to walk the dogs up and down Park Avenue and sometimes in Central Park. The dog walkers are young people, who, as they walk the dogs, are on their cell phones talking to other dog walkers (or dog pushers). The walkers are mostly from foreign countries. One young lady is from Ecuador. The only thing I know about Ecuador is that Lorena Bobbitt (who chopped off her husband's penis back in 1993 and became famous because of it) is from Ecuador.

The dogs are supposed to be good as "ratters" or guardian animals that track down mice, roaches, or small snakes, but this isn't true. The dogs are not good for anything, and even if a rat walked right past their eyes they would not pay attention. The dogs are virtually useless. Still, Nan loves them. Why?

Because she talks to them and they agree with whatever she says just so they're fed on time. I overhear her often as she talks to the dogs. She makes baby talk, as most elderly women dog owners do. They think they have babies when in fact they have dogs, and the women don't know the difference (or care), and so they just talk baby talk to the stupid dogs, and the dogs nod in agreement with whatever they're hearing, if they're hearing anything at all. I doubt they are. They're so self-absorbed, the dogs, that they are remote from all reality except their own fantasies, which center around food and have (as I already said) nothing to do with a sexual appetite.

The dogs do serve a purpose in our marriage, I guess, because when my wife talks to them she is less demanding of me—meaning: I do not have to listen to her during much of the day since she is talking to the dogs, and my attention is only minimally required. What I am trying to say is that dogs take a lot of pressure off our relationship. My wife talks to the dogs and is never verbally challenged by them—she just talks on and on, and she assumes they are agreeing with everything she is telling them. I, meanwhile, can read a newspaper or a book or can continue watching a sporting event on ESPN uninterrupted.

So the dogs are a positive addition to our home.

Barbara Taylor Bradford

A Woman of Substance, Barbara Taylor Bradford's first book, ranks as one of the top ten best-selling novels of all time. Her twenty-eight novels—all of them bestsellers here and in her native England—have appeared in forty languages and more than ninety countries, having sold over 89 million copies total. In 1999, she became the first living female author featured on a postage stamp, and the Writers Hall of Fame of America inducted her in 2003. We met her and her husband, Robert—who is German, like me, which gives us a special bond—at a dinner party in New York.

Robert and Barbara Taylor Bradford with Bijoux and Champagne

Our first bichon frise was a gorgeous dog with big black eyes as round as saucers in a fluffy white face. She was bright, cheerful, clever, and very intelligent, and she never failed to make us laugh at least twice a day. Her name was Gemmy, after all the Geminis in my life, even though she was actually a Scorpio!

When she died in 1992, my husband, Bob, and I were grief-stricken. We had lost our lovely little companion, who was twelve years old, and our homes seemed empty without her. After a couple of years, Bob wanted to get another dog, but I found the thought impossible. Then one day, four years after Gemmy's death, he became insistent, so I began to research bichon frise breeders in the New York area. I found several, talked to them all, and liked the sound of them. But only one had a litter about to be born.

In April 1996, about twelve weeks later, Bob and I drove out to see Mimi Winkler of Judges Choice Bichons at her home in New Rochelle. Of course within minutes we both spotted the puppy we wanted in the litter of beautiful bichons. She came trotting forward to sniff Bob's shoe and then looked up at us, her big black eyes so like Gemmy's. We both fell in love instantly. A *coup de foudre*, you might say, since she seemed to reciprocate our feelings. Naturally she came home with us that very day.

Bob wanted to call her Bijoux, after a dog he had owned before we were married, and I agreed. But she soon became Beaji, and that's the name she answers to, along with a number of other silly little nicknames.

One day, after Beaji had been with us for a few months, it struck me that she ought to have a little companion of her own so she wouldn't feel lonely, especially when we traveled. I telephoned Mimi, knowing she had another litter due any day. We went to see her after the puppies had been born, and once again we were lucky.

Another little ball of white fluff with big ebony eyes and a feathery tail came running out to inspect us and to sniff Beaji, whom we had taken with us. Of course it was love at first sight again for us all. We bought the second dog on the spot and decided to call her Champagne, because the name went so well with Bijoux and had a nice Parisian ring to it. But instantly she became Chammi and has remained so ever since.

Because we were about to leave for London, we boarded Beaji with Mimi so she could bond with Chammi, and bond they did. They're the best of friends and love each other very much. Beaji is undoubtedly the boss, though, the alpha dog. Always concerned about Chammi, she fusses around her like a mother! And they hate being separated from each other.

The day we bought Chammi, Mimi explained that the two dogs were related. They are cousins of a sort. They share the same grandfather, a Brazilian bichon called Gaspazinho, and Bob and I are certain that's why they look so much alike. In fact, the twelve-year-olds are identical except for size.

People who don't own dogs don't quite understand when Bob and I talk about the very different personalities of Beaji and Chammi. Beaji is quiet, steady, and a bit phlegmatic, always joined to my ankle, whereas Chammi is excitable, energized all the time, and tends to be slightly more independent. Like Garbo she often prefers "to be alone," and will sit in another room by herself. She also loves to jump from sofa to chair, sailing through the air, so I often say that she floats like a butterfly and kisses like a bee. Both dogs are affectionate, very sociable, and want to greet everyone, whether a friend, the butcher boy, or the UPS man.

Like Beaji, Chammi is bright as a button, intelligent, and clever, and both dogs understand so much. The two of them trot after me when I go to another room, and, just as Gemmy did, they make us laugh several times a day with their funny antics and their insatiable curiosity about everything.

These two adorable dogs bring love to our lives and life to our home. When I'm walking them, people often stop me and ask "Are they real?" because they're so beautiful. They are especially so when they shower us with little wet kisses and curl up next to us on the sofa. They are the best little companions in the world, and when I'm writing a book they keep me company under the desk so I'm never lonely.

Tommy Tune and Little Schubert

Tommy Tune

One of the most prolific and talented theater men of the past century, Tommy Tune has won a whopping eight Drama Desk Awards and nine Tonys for his acting and directing. He made his Broadway debut in *Baker Street* and his directing debut with *The Best Little Whorehouse in Texas,* and is known for his work on *Nine, My One and Only, Grand Hotel,* and *The Will Rogers Follies.* Ben knew him from the old Broadway crowd. I just saw his latest one-man show at the Regency Hotel, and, like a good wine, he really does get better with age. At six and a half feet, he's the real definition of tall, dark, and handsome, a beautiful man inside and out. One of the first contributors to this book, he believed in the project from the start.

Susan saw him first. She told Peter. Then Peter saw him, and he told me. I called the dreaded Marvin, my business manager. He said: "Do not get a dog until you finish your tour!"

Then I saw him, and the rest is his-story.

I was born in Budapest on May 18, 2002. I have blocked out the next few weeks, but I carry a vague memory of an overcrowded cage in the cargo section of a large aircraft and then—Hurray! I am plunked down in my own private cage furnished with a plethora of shredded newsprint—so comfortable. My roost lay atop a stack of other cages holding other immigrants. Alone in my little penthouse, I rehearsed my act carefully. I hid within the shreds so my cage appeared empty; then when a tall person peered inside, I made my surprise entrance, popping into view.

It worked with the tall, beautiful blonde (Susan). She was hooked, but she left me. Later, it worked with the tall blond guy (Peter). He could have been her twin, but he left, too. Oh, the anxiety! I told myself: *Just let go—let go.* But the wait was making me shake. Then came the tallest of them all, the dark guy with the smile. I thought to myself, *Stay hidden—make him think he's too late; make him think someone has already taken me from my newsprint bed.* I saw his smile fade . . . then I pounced! His nose was up to the cage. I licked the tip of it, and he was a goner!

Holding me in his arms, he walked me home from Pets on Lex NYC to his penthouse, which was considerably larger than mine and much higher in the sky. We spent our first night together huddled on his king-size Tempur-Pedic bed. Hey! I could get used to this; it's an upgrade from my shredded newsprint, and it smells good, too—like lavender and sandalwood.

The nose lick each morning as he opens his eyes has become my racket, the mainstay of my repertoire. It never fails to elicit his smile, which is better than applause to me.

He's happy, I'm happy; Susan and Peter are happy, and they visit me often. I'm so grateful to them for discovering me. The dreaded Marvin was miffed that my performance trumped his edict ("Do not get a dog until you finish your tour!"), but never mind. He's out of the picture now, and, as the famous Sondheim song goes, "I'm still here, I'm still heeeeeeere, I'm still heeeeeeeere." Woof, woof!

P.S. I don't want to brag, but there's a theater on 42nd Street that bears my name. They call it the Little Shubert. Woof, woof!

Robert Vaughn

Ben and Robert Vaughn filmed *The Bridge at Remagen* together in Prague in 1968, which put them right in the middle of it when the Soviets invaded and crushed the famous Prague Spring of freedom (page 56 [Havel]). Known for his lead role in *The Man from U.N.C.L.E.*, Vaughn, a prolific actor on both small screen and large, also appeared in *The Magnificent Seven, Bullitt,* and *The Towering Inferno.*

Robert Vaughn in the Man from U.N.C.L.E *days with puppy*

★

One day I saw my son, Cassidy, in the backyard with a very large dog. The dog was digging holes the size of manhole covers, one after another, with hardly a second between digs. The animal appeared to be in a frenzied state. When Cassidy came into the house with the dog, I asked him who owned the beast. He said he was simply minding him while the owner was visiting his parents, so I paid no further notice to the creature until about a week later, when I saw the dog sitting in the passenger seat of Cassidy's car, barking like a messenger from the outer circles of Hades. For several weeks, Cass and the Brown Bomber, as I called the dog then, came and went at will.

"What happened to the dog's owner?" I asked one morning.

Cass confessed that there was no owner—that he had seen the dog in a local pound and had inquired as to his well-being. He was told that if no one took him within a few days, he would be put down.

"So I took him," he said sheepishly.

"Does he have a name?" I asked.

"I named him Sam Adams."

I was impressed. "You named him after one of our founding fathers," I said proudly.

"No, Dad, I named him after the beer."

"Well, all right," I moaned. "And where does he go this fall when you go back to St. Lawrence?" I asked, referring to my son's college, located near the Canadian border, a seven-hour drive from where I live.

At that moment, Sam Adams slowly walked over to me and sat down, calmly looking up at me with his big, brown, soulful eyes. I knew there and then that I'd become the owner of a big and still-growing brown Labrador retriever. What I didn't know was that he would become a member of our family for nearly a decade.

Sam broke every harness and device our local vet and animal shop could provide. Finally, we got an iron chain used for towing cars, approximately sixty-five feet in length, and then drilled a hole in the front yard and drove a six-foot metal stake into it. In the back of the house, we got another piece of the iron chain and wrapped it around the bottom of a fat oak tree with a connecting chain that stretched to our kitchen door. This was Sam's playground, and play he did.

During the next large snowfall, I was away, and he managed one of his frequent breakouts, disappearing into the woods at the bottom of our property. My wife, Linda, armed only with a high-powered flashlight, finally found him tangled in the dark brush. Once she had freed him, he bounded away, knocking her into a deep bank of snow. She extricated herself, and, when she got back to the house, Sam was at the kitchen door, quietly and calmly waiting for his dinner.

On many occasions I, too, fell victim to Sam's hijinks, as we chose to call his looniness. Once, while I was tossing him a Frisbee, a FedEx truck came up our driveway behind me. As I was about to turn to wave at the driver, Sam charged, heading for the truck. He hit me at knee level, and I saw my feet against the sky before landing on my left shoulder, which broke. That wasn't the only outdoor event that played havoc with my limbs.

On the plus side, almost every night, Sam put his front paws on my chest as I sat in my chair, trying to catch up on world news. He looked deeply into my eyes, never blinking, until I took him out for his last nightly bark and toilette.

In 2003 I started a TV series in London entitled *Hustle*, requiring Sam to be boarded in Connecticut at a local doggy hotel named Cassio. Despite his ear-numbing barking, he was considered a splendid guest. Sam and I made the cover of *Healthy Pet* in the fall of 2006. He had beguiled and astonished the staff of that magazine with his boundless energy, herding the dozen or more deer that daily chowed down on our property. That was the last time I saw him at his barking, healthy best.

While Linda and I were in London, my daughter, Caitlin, training as a veterinary technician, visited Sam at his hotel. She noticed he wasn't well. *Hustle* had an autumn break that year, and when I got home I could immediately hear and see the difference in Sam. Though I didn't know it at the time, I took him for one last ride through our hometown. He tried barking but just didn't have the energy. He had developed multiple cancers.

As we were about to leave for the airport to return to London, I saw that my old friend was sniffing at his kitchen bowl, filled with all his favorite foods. He ate nothing. We knew we might never see him again, and it pained us to leave him. I knelt and we looked each other in the eyes. I think he also knew it was nearly over.

My dear Caitlin was with him when died. She said he went calmly, without a fight. From where I sit in my library writing this, I can see the canister containing his ashes. I noticed only recently, for the first time, that the bottom of the small vessel reads SAMUEL ADAMS, GAYLORDSVILLE, CT, NOVEMBER 22, 2006—my birthday.

Wim Wenders

We've been fans of German film director Wim Wenders and his work for years—the Palme d'Or-winning *Paris, Texas; Wings of Desire;* and *Buena Vista Social Club*—so Ben was very excited to have the chance to work with him on *Il Volo,* a 3-D film shot in Italy.

There was a time in my life when I dreaded Christmas. I tried to get as far away from it as possible. Australia seemed like a good place. It was summer there in December! And you couldn't be more removed from any place I knew than in the Australian desert.

I found myself waking up on Christmas Day in a little motel at the foot of Ayers Rock. You can't stay near the rock anymore; the whole area has been given back to the Aboriginal community, and Uluru is now sacred territory. Not yet in December 1977, though . . .

I was the only Christmas guest at the motel. It was already insanely hot in the morning. When I opened the door of my room, I could stare straight at Ayers Rock, sitting at the edge of my bed. I packed my camera, some water, and some nuts. When I stepped out into the blaring sun, it was six a.m. or so, utterly quiet except for the sound of crickets.

When I left the motel grounds, I met the dogs: two golden retrievers lying in the shadow of a eucalyptus tree. They got up as if they had been waiting for me and greeted me, their tails wagging. I patted them on their heads and then walked on. They walked with me, like an escort.

Wim Wenders pausing on the set of one of his movies

After a while, one of them stayed behind. When I turned around at the next bend, I saw him sitting in the middle of the red dust road, still looking after us. The other dog stood next to me and looked at me. He did not have that *Are you going to give me any food?* expression on his face. It was the *What are you going to do?* look.

"Well, let's go on," I told him, "if you feel like coming." I didn't have to ask him twice. He walked ahead. I followed him.

My plan was to walk around Ayers Rock on the northern side, take the recommended ascent from the east, climb down again, and return via the south side. It was damn hot. After an hour, the dog led me to a pond where he took a bath and then sat in the shade of an overhanging cliff. I took off my shoes and let my feet cool in the water.

Later on he took me off-road, on an almost invisible path through the bushes, and we ended up in a cave. When my eyes got used to the darkness, I saw the most amazing drawings on the wall: Aboriginal paintings, mythical figures, mysterious lines, maps. I took pictures. (Much later I found out that this cave was a woman's sanctuary; men weren't allowed in there. As I had no idea at the time, and there were no signs or warnings, I hope my transgression will be forgiven.)

The dog had been with me now for half the day already. Sometimes I lost sight of him, but he always found me again. He sat at the ascent to the Rock when I finally got there. It was noon and a hundred degrees or more, a merciless sun overhead. The dog looked at me with a certain curiosity. *I bet you're crazy enough to climb up there!*

I was. When I turned back, after my first hundred yards up, he sat in the only shadow at the foot of the rock and watched me. Then I lost sight of him.

I made it to the top. Nobody was up there. I didn't see a human being all day long. It was Christmas Day. Perfect!

When I came down in the afternoon, the dog got up and stretched. He wagged his tail again, clearly happy to see me, but didn't wait for a pat on the head. He immediately started walking home. He had a point. I had nothing more to drink, and we still had hours to go. We arrived back at the motel at sunset. The other dog stood at the gate, waiting for us. I sat on the fence and looked at them. They sat down on the road and looked at me. I laughed. They barked and walked away.

I went straight to the Coke machine, feeling very thankful. I had survived another Christmas without the blues, thanks to the nicest dog I ever met.

Stuart Whitman

Ben's second movie was called *Convicts 4,* and his costar was Stuart Whitman, known for his work in war movies and westerns. When I lived in Germany I remember seeing his handsome face in movies. A year before he and Ben worked together, Whitman starred with John Wayne in *The Comancheros* and earned an Academy Award nomination for his role in *The Mark.*

It was a warm Sunday morning a few years back, one of those mornings that reminded me of my childhood in Brooklyn, when we'd play hooky from PS 13 and find our way to Central Park in order to lie on the rocks and talk about the birds and the bees.

My fiancée and I were sitting on the deck surrounding our pool, just a stone's throw from the glimmering Pacific Ocean, reading the *Los Angeles Times.* She was poring over the fashion section, and I was enjoying the sports section, catching up on updates from Wimbledon.

Here at the ranch in Montecito, California, my land lay in front of me like the lone prairie. The riding ring was gone now; it went just after the horses. The dogs came, the dogs went. The chickens still lay their eggs, and all is well.

I was just about to close my eyes and enjoy a little nap when my fiancée handed me a section of the paper and said, "Look, honey—isn't he beautiful?"

Jet

Staring back at me was a picture of a bright-eyed, shiny black dog with perky ears. Underneath the picture ran the headline PET OF THE WEEK.

"Yeah," I said, "he is a good-looking fella."

Well, you can guess the rest.

I thought I'd convinced my soon-to-be wife that we didn't need a new dog, but still, she got me to saddle up my white Chevy Bronco, and we were off to the pound. *I'll just take the ride*, I thought, *because I've learned that no matter whether you decide to get one, or have a dog thrust upon you, they always take over.* I wasn't sure if I wanted to share my new wife, my lovely ranch, and my truck with someone else—especially someone with a wagging tail.

We arrived at the Humane Society and met the ladies there. I wasn't a complete stranger, since over the years my dogs had always somehow found their way off my land and into the hands of the authorities. The ladies and I spoke for a while, and everyone in the office talked over each other when I mentioned the Pet of the Week. Each person had her own story to tell about that dog. I could see that he was already a star in his own right.

Well, you guessed it. I went to the kennel and had a look. He was there among the yelps and barks, the handsomest Lab/pit cross you ever saw—not too big, not too small; just right.

On the way back to the ranch I explained to my new friend that things were different now and he didn't have to worry. I would look after him from now on. My fiancée was ecstatic. The only counsel I got from the girls at the pound was a firm reminder that this dog was a loner. He didn't need the company of any other dogs, and he would let any other dog know that right away. They made me promise to bring him back now and again for a visit.

He leapt from my Bronco and into our hearts. Fast as a comet, he ran around the trees and across the patio and down to the pool and into the field and back around again. Because of that we called him Jet.

He's a part of our family now, and part of the woodwork here at the ranch. His jet-black fur now ends at an appealing gray muzzle. He can still run like a bolt of lightning, but his penchant for fighting with the coyotes has run its course. When they come through nowadays, six or seven barks suffice. Having tended to two or three abscesses and a broken fang as a result of major altercations, he just wants to make sure they know that he's keeping an eye on their activities around the place. He protects us.

Franco Zeffirelli

Italian director and producer Franco Zeffirelli is best known for his Academy Award–nominated *Romeo and Juliet*. Other notable projects include his first film, *The Taming of the Shrew*, with Elizabeth Taylor and Richard Burton; the Mel Gibson *Hamlet*; *Tea with Mussolini*; and *Callas Forever*. He is also well known for his lavish opera productions, including the Metropolitan Opera's *Turandot*. From 1994 to 2001 he served in the Italian Senate. I adore Maestro Zeffirelli—not only because of his work as a director, but also for the lunches we enjoy with him at his villa on the Appia Antica. When in Rome, I always make it a point to get in touch with him.

Some years ago, I made a movie about the great soprano Maria Callas, called *Callas Forever*, which we shot in Romania. We used a beautiful baroque theater near a lake, and every morning we drove at least an hour to get there. On the road we saw what seemed like hundreds of dogs, too many of them lying dead on the side of the road. There were so many that the government paid two dollars to people for every stray dog they killed. Brigitte Bardot went to Romania to campaign against this horror, which was an ironic by-product of Romanians' love for dogs. They didn't spay or neuter the animals, so the country was full of them.

People love dogs in every country, but dogs need warmth and affection. They are a responsibility, and so often people, especially children, tire of the obligation, and the dogs feel it. Their biggest

Franco Zeffirelli and Bambina

fear is to be abandoned. I am adamantly opposed to considering a dog just another toy.

My studio had large windows that overlooked a gorgeous lake. One morning I had a visitor, a big, black, ugly dog. But the look in his eyes got to me, so I gave him something to eat and some water. Next day, he brought a friend who was prettier than he, but not as playful. Soon a honey-colored female joined the boys. I could tell by her distended teats that she was feeding, but there were no puppies with her.

Those visits went on for weeks until finally, twenty-five days later, the mother appeared with her five adorable pups. She came alone, without her friends. It was as though she were telling me she trusted me. I sat on the ground and petted and hugged the little animals as the mother looked on proudly. She was the only dog that Bambina, my Jack Russell and my best friend for thirteen years, didn't bark at. Bambina had been everywhere with me and had met many dogs, but this encounter seemed to please her most. She was allowed to approach and lick the tiny puppies as the mother looked on happily.

With me on the set morning, noon, and night, Bambina often lost interest and nodded off to sleep. The prop man had the idea to build her a sort of bed at the top of a sort of prayer kneeler. When it was time to start a scene there, we all forgot that Bambina was sleeping peacefully. Midway through a very dramatic aria, one of the secondary sopranos hit a very high note that Bambina didn't like. She poked her head out, which was very close to that of the soprano. The dog growled and let out a string of angry barks. Placido Domingo, who was in the scene, began to laugh. As a matter of fact, we all did. The soprano, on the other hand, fainted.

I had been feeding the big fellows, the mother, and her five children for weeks. Bambina became friendly with all of them. When we wrapped the movie and were set to leave for Rome, we saw all the dogs looking at us as though to say, *What will happen to us?* I had a decision to make: I could leave my new friends in Romania or take them with me to Italy. I decided, What the hell, let's take them home. I have plenty of room.

It didn't take me long to get permissions, vaccinations, and to have the dogs fixed. We had special traveling crates made for their trip to my villa on the Appia Antica in Rome. I'd started the picture with one dog, and now I had nine. But it didn't end there. Liz Taylor came by for lunch, carrying a small, adorable white Pekingese under each arm.

"For you," she said.

We had made a film together some time ago and got along very well. So it was her way to say, "I remember."

Epilogue: NEW YORK

My literary agent had just left our apartment with a draft manuscript of this book. We had decided it was time to start looking for a publisher. It was May 4, 2011, and Ben and I were sitting around, he in his easy chair and me with Maxi, our little dachshund, draped across my lap. We were making plans for the yearly getaway to our home in Italy. Then something happened.

"Ben," I said, "Maxi's heart is beating very hard and fast."

He reached over and placed his hand near her heart. "You're right. It seems to be racing away, and she's panting."

We called our vet, who told us to bring her in right away. By the time we got there, Maxi's heart had calmed down, and the panting had stopped.

"She seems all right to me," Dr. Blue said after examining her. "But I think we should do some tests, especially to check her calcium and cortisone levels."

The tests came back positive, which meant that Maxi was producing too much calcium from somewhere in her neck. They found a small tumor near her kidney.

"We should operate," the doctor said.

"And if we don't?" I asked.

"Maxi will crash within six months."

"How much time will the operation give her?"

"I'd say two and a half to three good years."

Ben and I looked at each other for a long time. I teared up. "But the anesthetic," I said. "Maxi is almost fourteen. Can she take it? Isn't it all too much for the little animal?"

"I'm sure she'll do well," said Dr. Blue.

Ben asked when he would do it.

"Bring her in tomorrow at eight a.m. In the meantime, I'm going to inject her with a mix of vitamins that will make her very happy."

When he brought Maxi back to us, she seemed much more alive, but she had a little bump on her back.

"What's this?" I asked.

"I call it a camel hump. It's the area I injected. It'll slowly disappear."

We said our farewells, making it clear how nervous we were. But what could we do? He was the expert, and we bowed to him.

It was a beautiful day, so we decided to take Maxi to her favorite spot in Central Park, the pond where children sail their little boats. As soon as we neared it, her tail started wagging, and she began pulling on her leash. She knew where she was going. During our walk more than one person stopped to pet her, saying how adorable she was, white snout and all.

We chose the uncrowded area around the pond, which had a grassy space where Maxi always enjoyed herself. Ben unhooked her leash and tossed her squeaky ball onto the grass. She ran to it with a speed she hadn't shown in quite a long time. Ben shouted "Brava, Maxi!" as I moved toward her. As soon as I joined her on the little hill, she pushed the ball to me with her nose. She was capable of sending it a long way. I picked it up and threw it. She chased after it, and the game began. Ben sat on a bench, watching and rooting. Back and forth went the ball for some time until I gave up, so Ben relieved me. Maxi was happy and tireless. It was like having our one-year-old puppy back in our lives.

How can this dog be dying? I remember thinking.

At precisely eight the next morning, we were back with the vet.

"We'll operate at ten a.m. As soon as she's stabilized, I'll give you a call."

In unison Ben and I told him to please take care of her.

"Don't you worry, Mr. and Mrs. Gazzara."

But we were very worried. We walked aimlessly around until Ben suggested that we go down to Chelsea to see a Picasso exhibition, and then maybe have lunch with our good friend John Martello at the Players Club.

The Picasso show was stunning. We got to the Players at one p.m., where John greeted us and escorted us to a table where two Bloody Marys were waiting.

"How did you know I'd need this?"

"Ben told me on the phone about Maxi."

"Aren't you having one?"

"You know, I think I will."

At that moment my phone rang. It was the vet. I picked it up before the second ring.

"Yes, Dr. Blue?"

"I'm very pleased, Mrs. Gazzara. Maxi is awake and resting on her sternum. Things went very well."

I looked across at Ben and raised a thumb. He looked at John, who shook his hand. They were beaming.

"Oh, thank God. No, thank *you*, Dr. Blue."

"Now you relax, and later in the afternoon a nurse will call to say when you can visit."

After lunch we went home. I was exhausted and decided to take a nap. Ben said he'd stand by the cell and home phones—that I should relax. I felt I'd been asleep for only a moment when Ben put his arms around me, lifted me into a tight embrace, and whispered, "Maxi's dead."

I wailed and screamed. "No, no, she's not dead! It went very well. Didn't he say that?"

"Her heart stopped. They couldn't bring her back."

"Where is she? I'm going to her."

"She's at the vet's, Elke."

"Let's go, let's go, let's go."

It was around five p.m. and there were no cabs to be had. My knees were going out from under me. Ben held me up as we waved for one off-duty cab after another. I was desperate, ready to step into the middle of Madison Avenue to stop one. That's when we heard a woman's voice call out to us, "Would you like this cab?"

An attractive young woman was inviting us to take the cab she'd flagged down for herself. As we got in I thanked her for her kindness. "I hope things will get better for you," she said, and closed the door, watching as we drove away. What a lady.

Ben was still paying for the taxi as I flew into the veterinarian hospital, met by someone I thought was a nurse but was herself a vet. She walked me to the back office, telling me everything had been fine up until 4:15 or so—that Dr. Blue had left her and her associate to look after Maxi. Not long after, her heart had stopped. They'd tried everything to bring her back, but couldn't.

Ben walked in as I was saying, "Dr. Blue should not have left."

"Mrs. Gazzara, he'd done all that he could. He felt that it was over, that Maxi would be all right."

"He should have been here."

Of course she changed the subject. "Would you like to see her?"

Ben and I looked at each other.

"No," I said. "I want to keep seeing her alive and happy."

"And no ashes," said Ben. "She'll be buried in our hearts."

That was it. I took Maxi's traveling bag, her leash, and halter, and we left the place. It was on the street that I broke down. Ben embraced me and suggested we walk home, that it wasn't far, and I agreed. Holding on to each other we crossed Third Avenue and headed for home. But on Lexington Ben stopped and looked around.

"What is it, Ben?"

"There's something I think we should do."

With that I found myself being ushered into a pet shop. I knew the place right away. I'd stopped in often, buying tasty treats and toys for Maxi. It's called Pets on Lex NYC, run by very nice people.

When I realized what Ben was up to, I grabbed his hand and headed for the rear where I knew the little puppies were kept. As we approached the cages, the yapping began, becoming louder and more desperate. The puppies were all colors. There were cocker spaniels, Yorkies, beagles—even tiny Chihuahuas. My eyes went to a miniature dachshund, the only dog in the place not barking. I was touched by its silence. It was as though it were resigned to remaining in that cage forever.

"Look, Ben. It could be Maxi. The same color."

"And the same kind expression," he said.

"Is that a boy or a girl?" I asked the salesman lurking behind us.

"A girl. Would you like to hold her?"

"Yes, I would. But will she suffer if we put her back?"

The fellow already had the dog out of her cage and into my arms. I caressed the little creature who held onto me as though saying, *Take me with you.*

"How much?" said Ben.

The man smiled. "They'll tell you at the desk."

After closing the deal, we received her papers. Our new family member was a thoroughbred from Missouri, whose father was named Maximus.

"Did you hear that, Ben? She was born in Missouri, just like Maxi."

"And her father's name."

We bought the best dried food they had and some canned meat in order to dampen it. The pup was teething, so we got her chew toys, and off we went. Ben carried Maxi's bag, and I carried our new little girl in our arms as we walked the six blocks to our home, holding each other tight around the waist.

Once back in the apartment, I sat where I'd last sat, holding Maxi. Ben poured himself a scotch and brought me a Diet Coke.

"What should we call her?" he asked.

"I don't know, Ben. We'll have to think about it."

"I always liked your middle name, Alma."

"No, that's too sad. It should be something happy and alive."

In all the time I'd held the little pooch in my arms, she hadn't made a sound. I rose and walked to the kitchen. As I poured cold water into one of Maxi's many bowls, I said, "She hasn't made a peep, Ben. Do you think she's frightened?"

"How about Stella?" he called out to me. "In Italian *Stella* means 'star.'"

I thought about that, and I liked it right away. Returning to the room I said, "She's going to spend a lot of time in Bell'Italia, where they pronounce the word so beautifully."

"Then it's a deal?"

I couldn't hold back a happy giggle. "It's a deal."

I looked across at my husband and loved him more than ever. "Thank you, Ben. I know you did this all for me."

"Like Mickey Rourke. You remember what he said in his story: If your dog dies, get another one right away."

I nodded and thought, *Thank you, Mickey.*

I knew Maxi was beginning to fade, but my mind had blinkers on. I wouldn't allow myself to think of a life without her. I must confess, I've cried more often for Maxi than I ever did for any friend. Is it because a dog's constant and unwavering love is what we search for but rarely get from a human being?

It was time to show Stella around the apartment. The lights were on in the den, so we started there. Maxi had always kept us company while we were watching TV, or when one of us was working at the desk, making herself comfortable on her big round pillow. I put Stella onto it, and she became agitated, sniffing hurriedly, and glancing up at us time and again. In our bedroom it was the same but more so. Maxi's main bed was there; she had slept with us always and got up only when we did. Stella was looking for her everywhere.

"Maxi sent her to us," Ben said.

Elke Gazzara and Stella

I picked the little girl up, kissed her warm snout, and told her, "We saved you, and you saved us. Welcome to the family, Stella."

Maxi died during the summer of 2011. It was unexpected, and we were devastated. My husband immediately got me little Stella, saying: "She is so beautiful and so young. She will be with you long after I am gone." He was right. Ben passed away just nine months later, in February 2012. Stella remained glued to him until the end, resting by his side like a sweet little angel; nothing could make her move. When the ambulance finally came to take him away, she kissed him so tenderly, so lovingly; it's as if she knew it would be their last good-bye.

My life was totally shattered. The only way I could overcome the emptiness, the potentially endless pain, was to work. It was probably the most difficult time I've ever experienced, but I decided right away that I would celebrate Ben's life as soon as I was able to accept the loss. I started to work on my book again, reconnecting with many of our friends, my co-authors, to complete the work, gathering permissions, photos, and the final few stories. It was a year full of details and memories, a year of positive distractions and a lot of healing.

I would like to extend my heartfelt gratitude and genuine thanks to every author, every friend who contributed a story to *No Better Friend*. I am forever grateful for your enormous support in helping me to complete this book, which is full of rich stories about love, life, loss, hope, and, most important, friendship.

Stella, by the way, is the most loving and precious gift Ben ever could have given to me. She is such a loyal friend and companion that I imagine I would be lost without her. She reminds me of our very special last summer together at our home in Italy. She was still a little puppy, chasing butterflies and salamanders. We couldn't take our eyes off her. We were so happy then, we three—Ben, Stella, and I. Now we two, Stella and I . . . we are never alone.

Acknowledgments

I would like to extend a very special thank you to my friend Douglas Ladnier, who helped me enormously. Also, big thanks to my agent, Jeff Ourvan, for all of his hard work. I am grateful for James Jayo and his editing expertise and kindness through the publishing process, and lastly thank you to my friend Don Weise for his encouragement and support.

About the Author

Elke Gazzara was born in Hannover, Germany. By age eighteen, she was a top model there, and her career soon blossomed into fame across Europe, China, and South America. After leaving modeling, Elke started her own skin-care line before going into the costume jewelry business, followed by a fun fling creating colorful, hand-knit sweaters for dogs—a delightful new opportunity to express her lifelong love for canines. She met award-winning actor Ben Gazzara while working on a film in Seoul, and after they married, they divided their time among New York City, the Hamptons, and Umbria. Ben chronicled their life together in his acclaimed memoir, *In the Moment*, and Elke recorded her life with Ben and their beloved miniature dachshund, Maxi, in the heartwarming *Madison Avenue Maxi*. Today Elke and her miniature dachshund, Stella, love to travel between Italy and New York City, where they visit Central Park every day in the beautiful memory of Maxi and Ben.